World
MYTHS

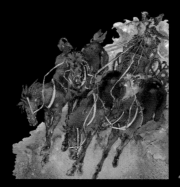

World Myths
was created and produced by McRae Books,
via de' Rustici, 5 – Florence, Italy
info@mcraebooks.com

Publishers Anne McRae, Marco Nardi
Text Hazel Mary Martell, Sarah Quie, John Malam,
Marion Wood, Rupert Matthews
Editors Anne McRae, Ronne Randall, Mollie Thomson
Illustrations Francesca D'Ottavi
Graphic Design Marco Nardi
Layout Vincenzo Cutugno, Ornella Fassio, Adriano Nardi
Cutouts Adriano Nardi, Ornella Fassio
Color separations Litocolor, Florence (Italy); R.A.F. Florence (Italy)

Printed and bound in China
International Standard Book Number: 0-88166-64-5

02 03 15 14 13 12 11 10 9 8 7 6 5 4 3 2 1

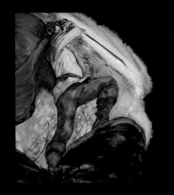

World
MYTHS

Hazel Mary Martell, Sarah Quie,
John Malam, Marion Wood, Rupert Matthews

McRae Books

Mesopotamian Myths 7

Marduk and the Babylonian Creation Myth • Gilgamesh and the Secret of Eternal Life • Utanapishtim Survives the Great Flood • The Marriage of Ishtar and Tammuz • Ishtar in the Underworld • Nergal and Ereshkigal • The Epic of Erra • Etana and the Eagle • Marduk and Nabu

Greek Myths 47

The Birth of the Gods • Cassandra's Gift of Prophecy • The Birth of Athene • Arachne the Weaver • Dionysos the Shape-Changer • The Siege of Troy • Daedalus and Icarus • Hades and Persephone • Poseidon and Pegasus

Egyptian Myths 27

The Creation • Osiris and Seth • Amun-Ra's Nightly Journey • The Battle for Kingship • Thoth brings Hathor Back • The Boating Party • The Magician • The Shipwrecked Sailor's Tale • How the Blessed Lived

Roman Myths 67

Aeneas, the Father of the Romans • The Wolf and the Twins • Claudia and the Great Mother • The Sacred Fire of Rome • The Slave Girls Save the City • Horatius and the Battle of the Champions • The Rape of Lucretia • Dido and Aeneas • Castor and Pollux – the Heavenly Twins

ANCIENT MESOPOTAMIANS

INTRODUCTION

The ancient lands of Mesopotamia are unfamiliar territory for many people. Yet they were home to the earliest civilization in the world. It was here that the first farmers learned to cultivate grain, growing what they needed rather than gathering wild varieties. They also tamed sheep and goats, keeping them for their meat, hides, and wool. The world's first cities grew up in Mesopotamia, and many of its earliest empires also flourished here. The peoples of Mesopotamia, who were among the first to use the written word, have left us many myths and legends. In this chapter, we have chosen nine of the best known stories.

MARDUK AND THE BABYLONIAN CREATION MYTH

At the very beginning of time, the two great gods Apsu and Tiamat existed alone. They created creatures to serve them – dragons and giant scorpions, fish-men and blood-drinking rams – and they created other gods as well. But soon these other gods began to annoy Apsu with their noisy talking and singing. He wanted to destroy them.

Ea, god of the rivers, learned of Apsu's decision. He called a meeting to warn the other gods and goddesses. None of them knew what to do, but Ea devised a plan and destroyed Apsu. Tiamat was furious and wanted revenge for Apsu's death, so she created an army of fearsome monsters. Both Ea and his father Anshar went forward in turn to do battle with Tiamat, but both were defeated. Then Marduk, son of Ea, spoke up. "I have a plan to defeat the monster Tiamat," he said. "But if I risk my life to save you, and succeed, I want you to make me king of you all." The other gods agreed.

Marduk prepared weapons of flames, lightning, winds, floods, and storms. When he challenged Tiamat to battle, she opened her mouth to tear at him, but before she could do any harm, Marduk released the winds. Tiamat tried to swallow them, but the winds filled up her whole body so that she could not close her mouth. Then Marduk shot an arrow into her stomach, which split her body open and pierced her heart. Marduk threw Tiamat to the ground and tore her body in half. One half he made into the Earth and the other half became the sky. Marduk formed the sky with stars, moon, and sun, and he set the length of the days, months, and years. Then he shaped the land into mountains, valleys, and hills. From Tiamat's eyes he made the Euphrates and Tigris Rivers. In the most fertile valley he created a place he would make his own. He called it Babylon.

GILGAMESH AND THE SECRET OF ETERNAL LIFE

After the death of his great friend Enkidu, the hero Gilgamesh of Uruk mourned deeply and began to fear his own death. Filled with grief, he roamed the countryside and set out to find the home of Utanapishtim, who was the only human to know the secret of eternal life. After surviving many dangers on his travels, Gilgamesh found Utanapishtim and asked him to share the secret of his immortality. Utanapishtim told Gilgamesh that, unlike some of the gods and spirits, all humans must die eventually. However, old men could become young again by eating a special plant of rejuvenation, which grew in the depths of the ocean. Utanapishtim warned that the plant was so covered in thorns that anyone who touched it would be cut badly.

Gilgamesh at once rowed out into the ocean in a boat, tied heavy stones to his feet, and leapt into the water. The stones dragged Gilgamesh to the bottom of the ocean where he saw the spiky plant. Gilgamesh grabbed the plant and suffered deep scratches, but he cut himself free from the stones and rose to the water's surface with the plant. He swam ashore and set out on his journey to carry the wonderful plant all the way home to Uruk.

On the way, Gilgamesh came across a spring of pure water. He stopped to bathe his bleeding hands. As he washed, a snake slithered out from the pool, snatched up the sweet-smelling plant in its strong mouth, and raced away with it.

Gilgamesh sat down and wept for his loss. "Was it for this that I toiled with my hands? Is it for this that I have wrung out my heart's blood? For myself I have gained nothing; not I, but the beast has joy of it now. I will leave this place and go." Sadly, Gilgamesh finally understood that he was not meant to be immortal. He returned home to Uruk, and when the city came into view, he saw the towering walls that he had built around the city. He realized that, even though he was destined to die as all people do, others would remember him for a very long time as the man who had created a magnificent city.

Resigned at last to his own mortality, the wise Gilgamesh continued to rule Uruk until death came to take him to join his friend Enkidu.

UTANAPISHTIM SURVIVES THE GREAT FLOOD

In the distant past, the great god Enlil, lord of the air, became very angry. He called together Anu, his father, Ninurta, his servant, and Ennugi, the god of canals. Enlil told them, "The uproar of mankind is intolerable and sleep is impossible." The other gods agreed, and they decided to destroy mankind. They sent for Adad, god of storms, and told him to create a mighty storm that would flood the entire Earth with water.

But the plot was overheard by Ea, god of the rivers that nourish mankind. He believed some humans should survive, and so he warned his favorite human, whose name was Utanapishtim of Shurrupak. He told Utanapishtim to build a large ship with seven decks and to load it with all his wealth, his family and servants, as well as seeds and pairs of every kind of animal. Utanapishtim did as he was told, and finished building the ship in just seven days. On the evening of the seventh day, Adad flew down from the hills and created a great storm. Heavy rain battered the land for six days and seven nights, and after this the entire Earth was flooded. By the seventh day, the storm had exhausted itself. The winds died down, and the waters quieted and began to recede. Utanapishtim released first a dove and then a swallow from the boat, but both came back. Finally he let a raven out, and when it did not return he knew that the bird had found somewhere to land.

Then Ishtar, the goddess of love, came to Earth and cried, "Alas, the days of old are turned to dust. Are these not my people?" The tip of a mountain then appeared from beneath the waters and Utanapishtim ran his ship onto the dry ground. After seven days, the flood waters receded. Utanapishtim opened the four doors of his ship and let all of the people and animals out.

Enlil was furious that any people had survived the flood. He came down to kill Utanapishtim, but Ea and Ishtar stopped him. Instead, Utanapishtim was taken away by the gods to live in a beautiful house where the rivers run into the sea. He and his wife were made immortal and given an endless supply of food.

THE MARRIAGE OF ISHTAR AND TAMMUZ

Ishtar, the goddess of love, traveled the Earth looking for a husband. One day she came across two men. One was named Tammuz, and he was the shepherd of the gods. The other was named Enkimbu, and he was the farmer of the gods.

Enkimbu was a strong man who looked after wide fields of beautiful grain and other crops. He had great wealth and had much to offer a wife. But Ishtar fell in love with Tammuz. Tammuz was tall and muscular, and he was the most handsome man that Ishtar had ever seen. Although he was poor, Tammuz was so good-looking that Ishtar chose him at once to be her husband.

After they were married Ishtar took Tammuz to her palace in the sky where they could live together and enjoy each other's love far away from the interruptions of gods or men. For many years all was well, but then Tammuz began to grow bored.

"You travel the Earth giving the gift of love to people and animals," he complained to his wife. "But I stay here and grow miserable without you. I need something to do."

Ishtar asked her husband what he wanted to do. Tammuz replied that when he had been a shepherd he had enjoyed hunting wild boar. "Allow me to go back to Earth to hunt boar while you are away," he begged. Ishtar refused.

"Why can you not be happy here where you are safe and away from the cares of the world?" she asked. But Tammuz continued to beg.

At last, Ishtar gave in. She gave Tammuz a spear and showed him how to return to Earth when she was absent. Tammuz enjoyed himself hunting on many occasions. Then, one day, he missed a boar with his spear. The enraged boar turned on Tammuz, threw him to the ground and ripped open his stomach with his tusks.

When Ishtar came home that day, Tammuz was missing. Ishtar searched for Tammuz and found him lying dead. Ishtar burst out weeping and cried, "Tammuz, Tammuz, I have killed you. Tammuz, Tammuz, you are no more." Ishtar was heartbroken and determined to bring her husband back from the dead. She set out for the Underworld.

ISHTAR IN THE UNDERWORLD

Ishtar, the goddess of love, was the most beautiful goddess of all. She was deeply in love with her husband Tammuz, a handsome shepherd. One day Tammuz was killed and taken to the land of the dead by Ishtar's enemy Ereshkigal, the queen of the Underworld.

Ishtar traveled to the Underworld to rescue Tammuz. When she arrived at the first gate she was met by Namtar, messenger of Ereshkigal, whose job was to collect the dead from the Earth.

"Before you pass this gate," said Namtar, "you must take off your crown." Ishtar did as she was told. They came to a second gate. "Before you pass this gate," said Namtar, "you must remove your earrings." Again, Ishtar obeyed the instruction. They passed through seven gates, and at each gate Ishtar was told to remove an item of jewelry or clothing. Finally she was completely naked.

The queen of the Underworld laughed. She had tricked Ishtar. Everyone was helpless in the Underworld if they were naked. Namtar sent sixty diseases to attack every part of Ishtar's body, and Ereshkigal threw her in prison.

Without the goddess of love, no crops would grow on Earth and no babies or young animals would be born. Ea, the god of rivers, realized what had happened. He created Asushu-Namir, a very beautiful man, and cast powerful magical spells to force Ereshkigal to obey instructions.

Asushu-Namir was sent to the Underworld. When Ereshkigal ordered him thrown into prison, Asushu-Namir uttered a magical spell. He ordered the queen of the Underworld to release her prisoner. As Ishtar walked back through each of the seven gates, she stopped to pick up her clothing and ornaments. When she reappeared on Earth she was as strong, beautiful, and as magnificent as ever. The crops started to flourish again, and the people worshiped Ishtar even more than before. But, although she was free, Ishtar had been unsuccessful in her quest to bring Tammuz back from the dead.

NERGAL AND ERESHKIGAL

One day the king of the gods decided to hold a banquet. Ereshkigal, goddess of the land of the dead, could not travel to the king's palace, and the king could not travel to the land of the dead. So it was decided that Ereshkigal's messenger should collect Ereshkigal's share of the feast from the palace.

But when the messenger arrived, Nergal, the god of disease, did not rise to greet him. When Ereshkigal learned of this she was furious and told her messenger, "I have been insulted. Bring Nergal to me so that I may kill him." The messenger returned to the palace and invited Nergal to the land of the dead to feast with Ereshkigal.

But Nergal's father Ea, the god of rivers, suspected a trick. He told Nergal, "When she offers you bread, do not eat it, for it is the bread of death. When she offers you water, do not drink it, for it is the drink of death."

When Nergal arrived in the land of the dead he was offered food, but he would not eat it. Then he was offered water, but he would not drink it. He was also offered a chair to sit on and a bowl in which to wash his feet, and he refused both of these things. Then he was offered a beautiful cloak, which he accepted and put on. Ereshkigal was furious that Nergal had avoided her traps, because she had fallen in love with him and wanted to keep him in the Underworld. But Nergal escaped.

Ereshkigal demanded that the gods return him to her, or she threatened to raise all the dead so that they would outnumber the living. So Nergal was sent back to the Underworld, with fourteen demons sent by Ea to protect him. The demons guarded the gate against Ereshkigal's monsters while Nergal leapt at the goddess. He dragged Ereshkigal from the throne by her hair and threw her to the ground.

Ereshkigal then cried out, "Do not kill me! Be my husband and I will grant you authority in the vast world of the dead." Nergal then bent down and kissed the goddess saying, "What you have been seeking will now be yours." Ereshkigal realized how much she loved Nergal. Together they ruled the Underworld and gathered people to their kingdom.

THE EPIC OF ERRA

E rra was the warrior of the gods and the commander of the Sebitti, seven gods of war who marched at his side when he went into battle. There had been peace in Babylon for a long time, but the Sebitti began to cry loudly that they were growing bored and old with no more battles. Erra's weapons complained, "We have become blunt, and rusty, and covered in spiders' webs, and we have almost forgotten how to fight! It is time for a war!"

Erra believed that Marduk had become a lazy ruler, allowing his people in Babylon to become too numerous and noisy, and he decided to begin a war in the city. But first he had to get Marduk out of the way.

"Your crown looks so battered and dirty," he told Marduk. "It is not fit for a god who rules a city as beautiful as Babylon."

Erra persuaded Marduk to go in search of the skilled craftspeople who could restore his crown to its original golden brilliance. The craftspeople lived far from Babylon, and Marduk was reluctant to leave his temple, not knowing what would happen if he was not there to protect his people. So Erra offered to stay in his place and watch over Babylon while Marduk was away. Marduk agreed and started on his journey. As soon as

Marduk had left the city, Erra began to spread devastation – he set families against each other, creating conflict and wars. Shrines, temples, palaces, and houses were destroyed in the fighting, and many people were killed.

Finally Ishum intervened and pleaded with Erra to bring an end to the destruction. But Erra would only stop the wars if the other gods accepted his demand that they become his servants. They had no choice but to agree.

21

ETANA AND THE EAGLE

When the city of Kish was still very young, the gods Enlil and Ishtar decided to find it a king. They chose the wise shepherd Etana. For many years Etana ruled well, but as he grew old he worried that he did not have a son to be the king of Kish after him. Etana prayed to Shamash, the sun god and god of justice, asking for a son. Shamash replied, "Take to the road and reach the mountain and ask an eagle to bring you the herb of birth from the home of Anu."

After a long journey, Etana reached the mountain and found a giant eagle lying in a ditch with his wings broken. Unknown to Etana, the eagle had been cursed by Shamash for eating the children of a serpent that belonged to the sun god.

Etana asked the eagle to help him find the herb of birth. The eagle replied that he would take Etana to the herb, if Etana would bring him food to keep him strong while his wings healed. After Etana had brought food to the eagle for several months, the eagle recovered his strength and was able to fly again. Etana climbed onto the eagle's back and they soared up into the sky toward the home of Anu. But as the eagle flew higher, Etana grew frightened and cried out, "My friend, I can climb no higher. Stop!" And so the eagle returned him to the ground. For several nights, Etana dreamed about flying high into the sky and of having a son, and finally he decided to try again. This time he was not afraid as the eagle ascended to the heavens, and together they succeeded in finding the precious herb of birth that would give Etana a son and heir to the kingdom. Etana returned to his city, and soon afterward he had a son named Balih, who became the king of Kish after Etana died.

MARDUK AND NABU

Once every year, the gods all gathered together in Upshukina, the palace of fate. There they discussed the destinies of men and women and argued about who should live and who should die, which people should be rich and which people should be poor. The final decisions were made by Marduk, king of the gods, but all the gods and goddesses took part in the discussion and put forward their arguments and opinions.

When Marduk reached his decisions, he whispered them to his son Nabu who carefully wrote the fate of each person down on his special clay tablet. When the time was right, Nabu checked the writing on his tablets to make sure of Marduk's orders. He then summoned the appropriate god, goddess, or demon, who was sent to Earth to carry out Marduk's instructions. Sin, the moon god, always stood close to Marduk during the discussions and sometimes he overheard Marduk's decisions or caught a glimpse of what Nabu was writing. Then Sin would send his messenger Zaqar to Earth to warn people of the fate in store for them. Zaqar moved through the night and whispered to people in their dreams. However, people did not always hear him correctly and sometimes misunderstood the voices in their dreams.

One year, Nabu came down from the palace of Marduk with his wife, Tashmetum. They lived on Earth for some time in the city of Borsippa. There Nabu and Tashmetum taught people how to read and write so that they could keep a record of the lives and destinies of men and women, just as Nabu wrote his own records of Marduk's instructions. Nabu and Tashmetum eventually returned to the heavens, but people have continued teaching each other how to read and write ever since.

ANCIENT EGYPTIANS

INTRODUCTION

Ancient Egyptian civilization flourished along the banks of the River Nile for almost 3000 years. It was one of the most brilliant and long-lasting civilizations in the ancient world. Even now, 2000 years after it faded into the Greek and Roman empires, it continues to fascinate. The Egyptians left behind more traces of themselves than any other ancient civilization, and Egypt's very dry climate has preserved them through the centuries. The Sphinx and many of the pyramids, mummies, death masks, papyri, and tomb paintings are still visible today. The beauty and exotic nature of Egypt's material culture is closely linked to its mythology. In this chapter, nine classic Egyptian myths have been adapted and retold for modern readers.

THE CREATION

In the beginning the black waters of Nun enveloped everything and there was darkness and silence everywhere. Then suddenly, out of the watery depths, the pointed tips of a closed lotus flower and a primeval mound appeared. Slowly, they both rose above the water until they were fully formed. The lotus flower then began to uncurl its tightly closed petals and a brilliant yellow light shone from it. When fully open it revealed the small, but perfectly formed figure of the creator, Amun-Ra, sitting in the blaze of light, surrounded by a wonderful perfume. He then turned into a beautiful phoenix bird and flew to the newly formed mound which was shaped like a pyramid. He settled down there stretching out his brightly colored red and gold wings and gave a great cry which echoed in the silence around him.

Amun-Ra became lonely in his watery solitude and so, out of himself, he created a son, Shu, the god of air, and a daughter, the lioness-headed Tefnut, goddess of the dew and of moisture. Amun-Ra was so proud of his children that he wept with happiness.

Shu and Tefnut then conceived a son, Geb, the earth god, and a daughter, Nut, the goddess of the sky. Geb and Nut cared deeply for each other and out of their love came four children. The first was a kind and honorable son, Osiris, who was followed by his brother, Seth. Lastly Nut gave birth to two daughters, the brave and magical Isis, and her gentle and caring sister, Nephthys. These children, unlike their ancestors, lived on earth. After them many more gods and goddesses were born.

Lastly, Amun-Ra ordered the ram-headed god, Khnum, to turn his potter's wheel and fashion man out of clay. Gently breathing life into man, Amun-Ra now realized that he required a place to live, and so he created Egypt. Just as Amun-Ra had emerged from the waters of Nun, so he created the River Nile so that Egypt and its peoples could grow and prosper.

OSIRIS AND SETH

As the Pharaoh of Egypt, Osiris ruled his country with wisdom and kindness. Osiris hated violence and he chose to civilize the Egyptians in a gentle manner. He showed them how to grow crops so that they could feed themselves. He taught them the law so that they learnt good and just behavior. Finally, he instructed them on how to worship the gods to ensure that Egypt prospered.

Things went well in Egypt until Seth, Osiris's wicked brother, who was deeply jealous of him, schemed to oust Osiris from the Egyptian throne. Seth held a lavish banquet and invited Osiris and all the gods and goddesses. During the evening Seth presented a magnificent wooden and gold chest to his guests and invited them to lie inside, promising that he would give it to the one who fitted it best. But Seth had slyly built the chest to fit only Osiris's exact measurements. When Osiris was persuaded to climb into the chest, Seth quickly slammed down the lid, sealed it, and threw it into the Nile where it soon drifted out to sea. The beautiful gilded chest became Osiris's coffin.

When Isis heard what had happened she searched far and wide for her beloved husband. After many months, she found his coffin in the palace at Byblos. Returning home with her gentle Osiris, Isis hid the coffin in the marshes in Lower Egypt. But one night, while she lay sleeping, Seth discovered the coffin. When he saw Osiris's body inside he became red with anger. In a violent rage he tore the body into fourteen pieces and scattered them throughout Egypt. Seth now believed that, at last, he was the only contender for the throne.

Then Isis learnt of Seth's savage behavior and, with the patience of great love, she began another long search, this time to gather the pieces of Osiris's body. Each time she found a piece, she built a shrine to honor her dead husband, tricking Seth into believing that she was burying his body. When Isis had collected all the pieces together she used her powerful magic to bring Osiris back to life for just one night. During the night they conceived their son Horus.

Now that Egypt had a legitimate heir to the throne, Osiris descended to the Underworld to rule as the King of the Dead. He showed the Egyptian people that, like him, they would have eternal life, and that their spirits, like his own, would live again after death.

AMUN-RA'S NIGHTLY JOURNEY

Every day the creator and sun god, Amun-Ra, spent twelve hours journeying across the sky in his solar boat. At night, taking the form of the ram-headed god, he descended into the dark, hot, windless depths of the Underworld in order to defeat the forces of chaos that were always threatening Egypt's stability. Every night his solar boat was towed through twelve different regions and in each one a demon waited to challenge his authority.

As the sun god approached each region his light blazed forth, awakening his enemies from their silent sleep. Cobras that spat fire and snakes with wings and many heads, were aroused during the twelve hours that it took Amun-Ra to travel across this deadly western realm to rise again, once more, in the east. The fiercest of all the monsters that attempted to destroy Amun-Ra was the snake Apophis. This wicked creature had no soul and was condemned to a life of chaos and evil. As the solar boat approached Apophis, goddesses leapt forward and slashed the snake with knives, leaving Apophis slithering and writhing in pain on the ground, as the boat passed him by. All the evil-doers, who were the enemies of Amun-Ra, were destroyed. They were shown no mercy; bound and decapitated they were thrown into pits of fire where their souls were burnt.

At the twelfth hour Amun-Ra reached his eastern destination. Taking the form of Khephri, the scarab beetle who emerged daily out of his ball of dung, he was reborn as the sun, signalling the safe arrival of a new day. Amun-Ra underwent this perilous journey through the Underworld every night. By completing the journey he showed he had triumphed over the dark forces that constantly threatened Egypt's very existence.

THE BATTLE FOR KINGSHIP

When Horus grew up he decided to challenge his wicked and cunning uncle Seth for the throne. Horus believed that, as the son of Osiris, he was the rightful ruler of Egypt. So he appealed to the gods, demanding that they make him pharaoh. But Seth was outraged, maintaining that as the strongest of all the gods he should be king.

After much discussion the gods decided to award Horus the throne. But Seth would not accept defeat and challenged Horus to a contest. Each god had to turn himself into a hippopotamus and remain submerged under the waters of the Nile. If either emerged within three months, he would lose the throne. But Isis, Horus's mother, feared for her son's safety. She was afraid that Seth would try to kill Horus under the water.

Isis threw a copper harpoon into the Nile, hoping to hit Seth. But it was Horus that leapt up. "Mother," he cried in pain, "you have hit me, your son!" Isis quickly withdrew her harpoon. Aiming once again she thrust it back into the Nile. This time she hit Seth. "Dearest sister," Seth cried cunningly, "Do not hurt me, your brother." At this, Isis once again withdrew her harpoon.

As Isis had ruined the first contest Seth challenged Horus again. This time they were to race down the Nile in boats of stone. Now it was Horus's turn to be cunning. He knew that stone could not float. So he built a wooden boat and covered it with limestone to make it look like stone. Seth foolishly made his boat out of a mountain peak, which sank as soon as it hit the water. Seth was

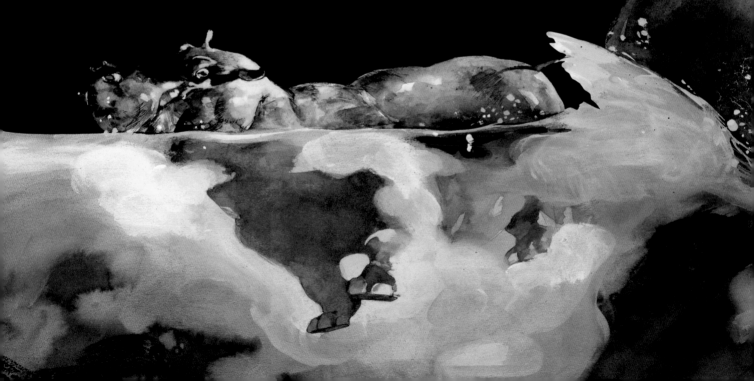

furious. How dare Horus trick him! Angrily Seth transformed himself into a hippopotamus and attacked Horus's boat.

Desperate to end the fighting between Horus and Seth, the gods finally turned to Osiris for advice. Osiris insisted that his son Horus was the rightful king and threatened to order savages from the Underworld to eat the gods' hearts if they did not respect his wishes. Fearing Osiris's wrath the gods immediately crowned Horus as the pharaoh of all Egypt.

THOTH BRINGS HATHOR BACK

One day the beautiful goddess Hathor quarreled with her father, the sun god Ra. She was so angry she turned herself into a lioness and left Egypt for Nubia where she roamed the countryside destroying and killing anything that dared to cross her path. When Ra learnt that his daughter had left he was deeply saddened; Hathor, the eye of the sun, no longer shone brightly in Egypt. So Ra asked his wisest and most learned scribe, the god Thoth, to go to Nubia and bring his lovely daughter home. On hearing Ra's request Thoth, knowing Hathor's wrath, feared for his life. After consulting his own writings and his book of magic, he decided to approach the goddess, not as himself, but as a lowly and meek baboon.

Thoth traveled south to Nubia and found the goddess. He tried to entice her back to Egypt with delicious fruits, delicacies and sweet memories of her home and her father. On hearing these the goddess began to weep for all that she had lost. Thoth invited her to accompany him back to Egypt and offered his protection during their journey. But the goddess laughed and ridiculed the little baboon, saying that he was no match for the power and strength of a lion. At this Thoth smiled and began to tell her the tale of the lion and the mouse. Although reluctant to follow Thoth, Hathor wanted to hear his tale, and so, slowly, the two of them made their way homeward.

"A fierce lion was raging through the forest," Thoth began, "trying to find a man to punish for all the cruelties he had inflicted upon the creatures of the forest. Hearing a shrill squeal beneath his large paw, he looked down to find that he was about to tread on a tiny mouse. The mouse begged the lion not to hurt him and promised that one day he might be of service. The lion roared with laughter at such a preposterous idea, but he let the mouse go free before going on his way. Soon afterwards the lion fell into a deep pit. A man came and bound his legs with leather straps and left him there to die. Suddenly, the little mouse appeared and, gnawing through the

straps, set the lion free. The lion was shamefaced in front of his new friend. He gathered him up in his mane, and the two set off towards the mountains." "Thus" concluded Thoth" "the smaller and weaker of the two helped the stronger." Hathor smiled gently, as they continued on their journey back to Egypt.

THE BOATING PARTY

Pharaoh Snefru was bored and restless. He was wandering aimlessly around his palace when he met his chief priest, Djada-em-ankh. Seeing the pharaoh's bored expression, the priest suggested that an outing on the lakes would refresh his spirit. "But choose only beautiful young maidens to row," the chief priest suggested, "for their beauty will combine with the loveliness of Egypt's green fields and shores, to lift your spirits."

Snefru agreed, and twenty of Egypt's most beautiful young women, with their hair newly braided and dressed in clothes of finely meshed fishnets, were selected to row Snefru across the waters using oars of ebony, gold and sandalwood.

Out on the lake, Snefru lay back in the boat, enjoying the gentle sweep of the oars in the water, the sweet perfume of the lotus flowers on the lake, and the beauty of the women rowing in unison. Suddenly, he heard a splash and then the women stopped rowing. When he asked what was wrong, one of the maidens, the chief rower, cried out that her beautiful new turquoise pendant had fallen into the water. The pharaoh, seeing how distraught she was, told her not to worry and to keep on rowing because he would give her a new pendant. When she refused, Snefru was furious. He summoned Djada-em-ankh and insisted that the chief priest use his magical powers to restore calm to the boating party. So Djada-em-ankh divided the waters in two like a blanket and folded one half back upon the other. Looking down at the bottom of the lake, Djada-em-ankh spotted the turquoise pendant lying on top of an old broken piece of pottery. Quickly retrieving it, he returned the pendant to its owner and,

uttering another magic spell, restored the lake to its original calm. Snefru was so delighted by these events that he invited everyone to a magnificent feast at the palace that evening.

THE MAGICIAN

One day Pharaoh Khufu was bored and so he invited his son, Prince Hardedef, to tell him a magical story. Instead, the Prince told his father of a real magician called Djedi. "He is 110 years old and lives in a town called Djed-Snefru," Hardedef told his father. "He is, moreover, famed not only for his huge appetite, for he eats 500 loaves of bread and half an ox a day, but also for his ability to tame wild lions and to join the severed heads of wild creatures. It is also said that he knows how many secret rooms there are in the chamber of Thoth." At this Khufu became excited and commanded Hardedef to bring Djedi to the royal court, for the

pharaoh wanted to copy the secrets of Thoth's sanctuary into his own tomb.

At his father's request, Hardedef brought Djedi to the palace to meet him. The pharaoh inquired whether it was true that Djedi could reunite the heads and bodies of decapitated animals. When Djedi said that it was true, a goose was brought to the court and killed. Its head and body were then placed at opposite ends of the room. Djedi uttered his magic spells and the goose's body and head suddenly began to move towards each other. Before a spellbound audience, its body joined its head and the goose, now alive, cackled noisily. Then an ox and a long-legged bird were brought into the court and the experiment was repeated. Once again, both creatures were brought back to life when Djedi performed his magic.

Fascinated, Khufu now asked the question that really interested him. "Tell me, how many secret chambers are there in the Sanctuary of Thoth?" Djedi replied that the answer could only be given by the eldest child of Ruddedet – the wife of a powerful priest – who would, one day, rule Egypt.

On hearing this prophecy Khufu grew sad, fearing that his family would lose the Egyptian throne. But when Djedi told Khufu that his own son and grandson would rule Egypt before Ruddedet's children, Khufu smiled again. Knowing the magician's passion for food the pharaoh then rewarded Djedi with 1000 loaves of bread, an ox, a mountain of vegetables and 100 jugs of beer.

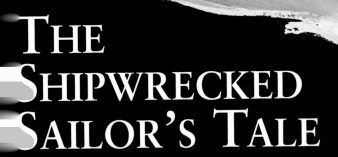

THE SHIPWRECKED SAILOR'S TALE

My story begins with a trading expedition that I led to the royal mines of the Red Sea. My large ship had a crew of 120 of Egypt's most experienced sailors. Yet we never arrived at our destination. For suddenly a violent storm arose and colossal waves smashed the mast. The boat capsized and I was thrown overboard.

I awoke to find myself marooned, alone, on an island. I was so frightened that I hid among the trees. For three days I ate nothing. Then, desperately hungry, I decided to explore my new home. To my surprise I found wonderful things – figs, grapes, date-palms, cucumbers, fish and birds. I had landed on an enchanted island! Joyously, I lit a fire and gave offerings in thanks to the gods. But suddenly the ground began to move. There was something coming towards me. I froze in terror. As it moved closer I saw that it was a giant golden snake.

Rearing up its head the snake demanded, "What are you doing here?" Then to my horror it picked me up in its jaws and carried me to its pit. Gathering my courage I told my tale. Suddenly, the snake became friendly. I would be rescued in four months' time, he told me. "If this is true," I replied "I shall send you a valuable cargo from Egypt." The snake laughed. "It is I, not you, who is the Prince of Punt!" he said. "My island contains treasures beyond your reckoning. When you leave I will give you such a precious cargo that the pharaoh will richly reward you."

After four months I was rescued and

the snake, true to his word, gave me valuable treasures. The pharaoh, delighted with my booty, made me a palace official. The snake's prophecy had been fulfilled.
But I have never been able to visit the island again, for it has mysteriously disappeared.

HOW THE BLESSED LIVED

The Egyptians believed that after they died they would go to an idyllic and prosperous Afterlife in the Elysian Fields. These fields would be surrounded by canals and fruit-laden trees and the air would be fragrant with the perfume of flowers and incense. No longer would the Egyptians have to worry about the Nile flooding too much and ruining their crops or flooding too little, causing drought and famine. Instead the canals would irrigate the rich and fertile Egyptian soil and an abundance of barley and emmer wheat would grow. Wine, beer and milk would flow and cakes, oxen and ducks would be eaten. No longer would the Egyptians toil every day in the hot sun behind their ox-drawn plows; instead shabtis, magical servant figures, would labor in the fields.

In the Afterlife the Egyptians would spend their time singing, playing games, sailing down the Nile, hunting for birds and fishing in the marshes, feasting, and making offerings to the gods, all among friends and family once more united.

But to reach this prosperous and golden Afterlife every Egyptian knew that their spirit had to face a perilous journey when their behavior on earth would be judged. The Judgement of the Soul took place in the Hall of Two Truths where Osiris, seated upon his throne, was surrounded by forty-two judges all carrying sharp knives. On reaching the hall the deceased had first to plead not guilty to crimes such as murder and stealing. Then, showing great courage, the dead person had to address the gods by their individual names and make further statements about their good behavior. "O Bone-Smasher who comes from Hnes; I have not told lies," and "Oh Blood-Eater who comes from Slaughterplace; I have not slain sacred cattle." Finally the deceased's spirit had to give a great shout of "I am pure, I am pure, I am pure."

The next stage of the judgement was even more terrifying. Anubis, the jackal-headed god, weighed the deceased's heart against the feather of truth. If the heart and the feather did not balance, the Devourer, an ugly creature that was part lion, part hippopotamus and part crocodile, stood by eagerly waiting to eat the deceased's heart. If found pure, the deceased would be taken to Osiris and the doors to the Elysian Fields would be opened and they would walk out into the land of the blessed.

ANCIENT GREEKS

INTRODUCTION

The ancient Greeks left us a very rich legacy of stories inspired by their gods, goddesses, and heroes. These myths were adopted by the ancient Romans, who displaced the Greeks in power in the Mediterranean world. These stories and the Greeks' civilization have been admired and retold ever since and have had a profound influence on the formation of Western culture. It is hard to imagine what European poetry or theater would be like if the Greeks had never existed. Would the explosion of art and learning from the 14th to 16th centuries, which we now call the Renaissance, have taken place if all trace of Greek civilization had vanished? The Greeks also invented democracy and the modern alphabet, and laid the foundations of mathematics, philosophy, astronomy, and medicine. In this chapter, nine of the best loved Greek myths have been beautifully retold for modern readers.

THE BIRTH OF THE GODS

The ancient Greeks believed that, before the gods were born, the universe was in a state of chaos. Gaia, or Earth, emerged from this chaos and gave birth to a son called Uranos, or Sky. She then married him and they had many children. The first to be born were monsters and giants, including the three Cyclopes who only had one eye each, but Uranos banished them from Earth because they were so ugly. Gaia then gave birth to seven Titans and seven Titanesses. They were also giants, but shaped like humans.

Angry over the way Uranos had treated their first children, Gaia encouraged the Titans to rebel against him. They were led by Cronos who attacked his father with a sickle and took over his power. During the attack, however, three drops of Uranos's blood fell on the earth and turned into three creatures known as the Furies, while another drop fell into the sea where it turned into the foam from which Aphrodite, goddess of love and beauty, was born. Cronos then married his sister, the Titaness Rhea, and had five

children with her. But, because he had been warned that one of his children would overthrow him, Cronos swallowed each child at birth. Not wanting to lose her sixth child in this way, Rhea wrapped a stone in baby clothes and Cronos swallowed that, while the real child, Zeus, was hidden away and brought up by the Nymphs.

When he was old enough to face his father, Zeus put on a disguise and went back to his home. He gave Cronos a magic potion which made him cough up his three daughters, Hestia, Demeter, and Hera, and his other two sons, Hades and Poseidon. Unharmed by the experience, Hades and Poseidon then joined forces with Zeus in the struggle against their father. Zeus brought back the Cyclopes which Uranos had banished and they fought with him, while the Titans fought with Cronos.

The battle between the two sides was long and fierce, but eventually Zeus and his followers defeated Cronos and the Titans and banished most of them to the Underworld. Zeus then became king of all the gods, who were known as the Olympian gods because they lived on Mount Olympus. He married his sister Hera, with whom he had several children, but he also had many more children with other goddesses, mortals and even Titanesses. His brother Poseidon became the god of the Ocean, while Hades became the god of the Underworld.

Cassandra and the Gift of Prophecy

Cassandra was one of the daughters of King Priam of Troy and his wife, Hecuba. Her brother was Paris, whose kidnapping of Helen, the beautiful wife of the Spartan king Menelaus, led to the outbreak of war between Greece and Troy. Cassandra herself was so beautiful that the god Apollo fell in love with her, even though she was a human and not a goddess. He offered her the gift of prophecy in exchange for the promise to marry him. Cassandra accepted Apollo's gift, but then went back on her promise and refused to have anything more to do with him. Angry and disappointed with her, he decided to turn the gift into a curse. Although Cassandra would still be able to predict the future, no one would believe what she said.

Her most important prediction was made while the Greeks were besieging the city of Troy. When the Greeks sent in a large wooden horse as a gift, Cassandra could see that it was a trick that would lead to the downfall of the city. She tried to warn the Trojans, but, as a result of Apollo's curse, not one of them believed her. Their city was overwhelmed and Cassandra herself was taken prisoner by Agamemnon, who was the king of Mycenae and the brother of Menelaus. He was also the husband of Helen's sister, Clytemnestra, but she had been forced to marry him against her will.

Cassandra became Agamemnon's slave and bore him twin sons before returning to Mycenae with him. On the journey to his home, she told Agamemnon that Clytemnestra was planning to murder him. But once more she was not believed and, as Clytemnestra gave Agamemnon a warm welcome and prepared a bath for him, it seemed that Cassandra was wrong. While her husband had been away, however, Clytemnestra had found a lover, Aegisthus, and together they had set a trap for Agamemnon. As he climbed out of the bath, Clytemnestra pretended to be handing him a towel, but in reality she had a net in her hands and threw it over him so that he could not move. Aegisthus then came into the room and stabbed Agamemnon to death, while Clytemnestra killed Cassandra and her two baby sons.

THE BIRTH OF ATHENE

The goddess Athene was the daughter of Zeus and Metis, who was the Titaness of wisdom. But, before Athene was born, Zeus was told that any son born to Metis would grow up to be more important than his father. Not knowing whether the child that Metis was expecting would be a girl or a boy, Zeus decided to solve the problem by changing Metis into a fly and swallowing her. Shortly afterward, however, while he was out walking with Hephaestos, the blacksmith to the gods, Zeus began to suffer from a terrible headache. He told Hephaestos to hit him on the head to relieve the pain. Hephaestos obeyed and for a moment Zeus's skull cracked open and out stepped the adult Athene, dressed in armor and ready for battle.

She carried a spear and a shield and wore a helmet, but because she had inherited wisdom from her mother, her symbol was the owl. This wisdom led her to try to solve arguments by reasoning, rather than by fighting, though the people she supported in warfare always won their battles.

One of Athene's own greatest arguments was with Poseidon, the sea god, as she wanted the most important town in Greece to be named after her, while he wanted it to be named after him. The people of the town suggested that Athene and Poseidon each make a practical gift to the town and the inhabitants would then name the town after whoever had come up with the most useful idea.

The town was built around a rock known as the Acropolis. Poseidon hit it with his trident and a stream started to pour out, quickly giving access from the town to the sea. Then Athene touched the same rock with her spear and the first olive tree sprang out of the ground. As well as providing food, its fruits could be crushed to make oil for lighting and cooking. The townspeople realized that this was not only useful for them, but could also be exported in exchange for gold, silver or other goods. This made them decide that Athene's was the better gift and so they named their town Athens after her. A shrine known as the Parthenon was built for her on top of the Acropolis and Athene then became their special goddess and guardian of their town.

ARACHNE THE WEAVER

In ancient Greece most women knew how to spin wool into yarn and cloth, but not one of them was as skilled as the princess Arachne. She could take the finest thread and weave it into the most delicate cloth. Unfortunately, she was rather conceited and liked to boast about her skills. One day she even boasted that she could weave better than Athene who was the goddess of home crafts, as well as being the goddess of wisdom and war.

Athene was also proud of her weaving skills and, when she heard of Arachne's boast, she challenged the princess to a weaving contest. Arachne accepted the challenge and she and Athene set up their looms. Neither the goddess nor the princess looked at each other as they wove their cloth. Instead, they both concentrated on doing their very best work. The goddess thought she would win easily and at the same time teach Arachne not to be so boastful in future. When they had finished, however, Athene was horrified to realize that the length of cloth that Arachne had woven was every bit as beautiful as the one she had woven herself. Overcome with jealousy and anger, she ripped Arachne's cloth from the loom and tore it into shreds.

Arachne was terrified by Athene's anger and, realizing that the goddess would never forgive her, she ran from the room and hanged herself from a tree. Athene chased after her, but when she saw what Arachne had done, the goddess's anger melted away and she felt ashamed of herself for behaving so badly. Taking pity on Arachne, Athene decided to bring her back to life again so that her weaving skills would not be lost. But the goddess still could not bear the thought of any mortal being a better weaver than she was and so, rather than make Arachne human again, Athene turned her rival into a spider who would spend the rest of her life spinning fine thread and weaving it into beautiful webs.

DIONYSOS THE SHAPE-CHANGER

Dionysos was both the god of wine and the god of the theater. His father was the god Zeus and his mother was Semele, the daughter of the king of Thebes. When she was expecting a child, Semele was tricked by Zeus's jealous wife Hera into asking Zeus to reveal himself to her in all his glory. Knowing that seeing him in this state would mean instant death for Semele because she was a mortal, Zeus was reluctant to agree to her request, but eventually he was persuaded to appear in his heavenly chariot, surrounded by thunderbolts and lightning. Semele took one look and was turned to ashes, but Zeus saved the child she was expecting and it became Dionysos.

As Dionysos grew up, he was cared for by Silenus, one of the less important gods who spent most of his time on earth. Silenus enjoyed life to the full, however, and often acted irresponsibly. He liked to

get drunk and his companions, known as the Satyrs, enjoyed chasing girls. Together with Dionysos, they traveled around the world, having a good time and spreading the knowledge of making wine from grapes. They often annoyed people, however, and Dionysos sometimes had to get out of trouble by changing from human form into an animal.

On one of his adventures, Dionysos hired a ship to take him from the port of Icaria to the island of Naxos. But, unknown to him, the ship belonged to pirates and, once they had him on board, they planned to take

him to a foreign country and sell him as a slave. To prevent his escape, they tried to tie him up with a rope, but the knots would not stay fastened. Then Dionysos used his powers to turn their oars into snakes and make vines and ivy grow around the masts of the ship so that the sails could not be hoisted. When the pirates still refused to release him, he turned himself into a ferocious lion and chased them around the ship until they all jumped into the sea. There they were turned into dolphins, while Dionysos returned to his normal shape and continued his journey.

THE SIEGE OF TROY

When Paris, the King of Troy's son, abducted Helen, the wife of King Menelaus of Sparta, and refused to return her to her husband, the Greeks declared war on the Trojans. Led by Menelaus's brother, Agamemnon, they gathered a fleet of a thousand ships and set sail for Troy. By the time they got there, however, Helen had enchanted all the Trojans with her beauty and charm and they were prepared to fight the Greeks rather than give her back to them. Fortunately for the Trojans, Troy had thick walls and strong gates but, although the Greeks besieged the city, their army was not powerful enough to drive the Greeks away. The siege went on for ten years and men were killed on both sides, but neither the Trojans nor the Greeks would give up the fight. Then Odysseus, King of Ithaca and the Greeks' chief warrior, thought of a way to trick the Trojans into letting the Greek army into their city.

Following Odysseus's instructions, the Greeks built a huge wooden horse, but it was hollow, with enough space inside for several armed warriors. The warriors got into the horse and it was placed outside the gates of Troy. All but one of the other Greek warriors then went to their ships and started to sail away. The Trojans saw this and thought the Greeks were giving up. They also saw the horse and the one Greek warrior who had been left behind. He told them that, if they took the horse into Troy, it would protect the city for ever. Paris's sister, Cassandra, tried to warn the Trojans against this, but they would not listen. They pulled the horse through the gates and began to celebrate their victory. When darkness fell and the Trojans went to their beds, the Greek warriors climbed out of their hiding place and quickly opened the gates of Troy to let in the rest of the Greek army which had been waiting just offshore. The Trojans were defeated, their city was ransacked and Helen was captured and returned to Menelaus.

DAEDALUS AND ICARUS

Daedalus was a skilled craftsman and inventor who lived in ancient Athens. He was a member of the royal household and had a son called Icarus. He had a nephew called Perdix who was also an inventor. When Perdix claimed to have invented the saw, however, Daedalus was overcome with jealousy. He killed Perdix by throwing him over a cliff, then fled into exile on the island of Crete, taking Icarus with him.

Crete at that time was ruled by King Minos. He had asked Poseidon, god of the sea, to give him a bull which he would then sacrifice to the god. But when the bull arrived, it was so magnificent that Minos did not want to kill it. Instead he tried to sacrifice another bull in its place. This angered Poseidon so much that, for revenge, he made Minos's wife, Pasiphae, fall in love with the bull. Taking pity on her, Daedalus helped Pasiphae to meet the bull by building a beautiful, life-size model of a cow with enough room inside for her to hide. As a result of this meeting, however, Pasiphae gave birth to the Minotaur, a fierce creature which was half-human and half-bull.

As the Minotaur grew up, it became fond of eating human flesh and terrorizing people, so Minos instructed Daedalus to do something to keep it under control. So Daedalus built a complicated maze, known as the Labyrinth. Once it was put in the middle of the Labyrinth, the Minotaur could not find a way out and had to stay there for the rest of its life.

Then Daedalus fell out of favor with Minos and ended up in prison himself. Icarus was with him and, realizing that Minos would kill them both, Daedalus thought up a way of escape. Using wax and feathers, he made a pair of wings for Icarus and another for himself and together they flew out of the window.

Daedalus warned Icarus not to go too near to the sun because of the wax in his wings, but once he was in the air, Icarus found that he liked flying so much that he forgot his father's warning. He flew higher and higher, until suddenly the wax melted and his wings fell apart. Icarus plunged into the sea and was drowned, leaving Daedalus to fly on alone to a new life on the island of Sicily.

HADES AND PERSEPHONE

Hades was the god of the Underworld. He was very rich but very lonely because nobody wanted to live in his dark and gloomy kingdom. Sometimes he visited the earth just to look at the people there. On one of his visits he saw Persephone gathering flowers in a field and fell in love with her. She was the daughter of Demeter, the goddess of plants and harvests. The two of them were very close and Persephone often helped Demeter in her work.

Realizing that Demeter would never give him permission to marry Persephone, Hades decided to abduct her. He grabbed her by the hair and pushed her into his chariot, then raced back to the Underworld with her. Not knowing where her daughter had gone, Demeter neglected the earth and set out to look for her. The flowers withered and the leaves fell from the trees. The crops stopped growing and the people started to go hungry. Then, when she found out what had happened to Persephone, Demeter asked Zeus to help her. He told her that Persephone could return to the earth, providing she had not eaten anything while she was in the Underworld, and he sent Hermes the messenger to command Hades to set her free.

Meanwhile Persephone had been refusing to eat. But when Hades offered her twelve juicy seeds from a pomegranate, she found she was too hungry to resist. When Hermes arrived, she had already eaten six of them. Hades said that meant she would have to stay with him for ever, but Zeus intervened. He said that because Persephone had only eaten six seeds, she only had to spend six months of every year in the Underworld. For the other six months she could return to the earth and be with her mother. Demeter agreed and, while Persephone was with her, she tended the plants and made them grow. When her daughter had to go back to the Underworld, however, Demeter let all the plants wither and die and did not tend them again until Persephone came back to her.

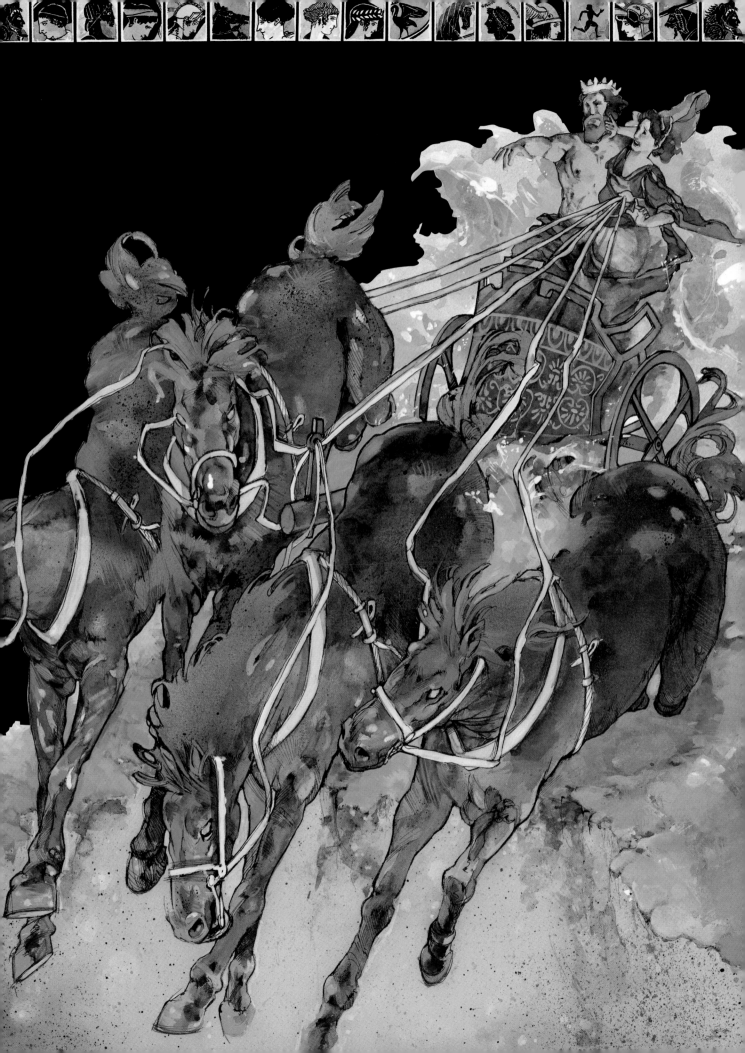

POSEIDON AND PEGASUS

Poseidon was the god of the sea and the brother of Zeus and Hades. He had control over all the sea monsters and could calm storms by riding over the sea in his golden chariot which was pulled by a team of white horses. He could also cause earthquakes by striking the ground with his trident. His many offspring included giants and monsters, as well as mortals and the winged horse, Pegasus.

The mother of Pegasus was Medusa, one of the Gorgons. She met Poseidon in one of Athene's temples. This angered Athene so much that she turned Medusa's hair into snakes and made her and her two sisters into monsters who would turn into stone any mortal who looked at their faces. Later, Athene helped Perseus, the mortal son of Zeus and Danae, to kill Medusa by giving him a polished shield in which he could see Medusa's reflection while keeping his back turned to her. Athene also gave Perseus a crystal sword with which he could cut off Medusa's head. When he did this, Medusa's blood spilled on the ground and Pegasus sprang out of it.

Unlike his mother, Pegasus was good-natured and obedient, doing as he was told by either Athene or Poseidon. When the mortal Bellerophon was sent to kill the fire-breathing monster known as the Chimaera, Pegasus was sent to help him. Bellerophon climbed onto his back and Pegasus flew with him far enough from the Chimaera for its fire not to burn them, but close enough for Bellerophon to plunge his spear down the Chimaera's throat.

Unfortunately Bellerophon enjoyed flying on Pegasus so much that he decided to use him to fly to the gods' home on Mount Olympus. As no mortal was allowed to go there without an invitation, Bellerophon's action made the gods very angry. Zeus decided to punish him by sending a fly to bite Pegasus under his tail. Pegasus went wild with the pain and, as he reared up, Bellerophon was thrown from his back and went crashing back to earth. Pegasus himself became one of Zeus's servants and eventually turned into a group of stars shining in the night sky.

ANCIENT ROMANS

INTRODUCTION

The civilization of the Romans spanned more than 1,000 years. From modest beginnings in a region of northern Italy, the empire of the Romans spread out to cover many parts of Europe, North Africa, and the Middle East. Within this vast area lived millions of people who came under Roman rule. Some had been conquered in battle by the Roman army; others had accepted the Romans without a struggle. The Romans spread their culture far and wide. Roman coins made in Britain or France could be spent in Spain and Greece, Israel and Egypt. The Roman language, Latin, became the first international tongue – just as English is today. It was in Latin that the myths of the Romans were first spoken and written, telling tales about the history of the Roman people, and of Rome – the city that was the heart and soul of the Roman world.

AENEAS, THE FATHER OF THE ROMANS

Long ago, the citizens of Rome told a story about a warrior from the east who came to live in the land of the Romans. His name was Aeneas, and for them he was the father of the Romans.

The story of Aeneas begins when the goddess Aphrodite came to Earth. She visited Phrygia, that part of the world where Turkey is now, and where the city of Troy once stood. Aphrodite walked among the human race and fell in love with King Anchises.

She bore him a son, whom they called Aeneas. The young Aeneas was cared for by nymphs, but when he was five years old Aphrodite took him away and gave him to his father. Overcome with joy, Anchises boasted that Aphrodite was the mother of his son. On hearing this, Zeus, the ruler of all gods, grew angry. He threw a thunderbolt at Anchises, striking him on the leg and making him lame.

There came a time of war, when soldiers from Greek cities attacked Troy. After ten years of fighting, Troy fell to the Greeks. They invaded the city and set it on fire. Aeneas knew this was the end – there was nothing he could do to save the city. Carrying his aged father on his back, and his young son in his arms, Aeneas escaped to the safety of nearby mountains. For many months they lived there with other survivors from Troy. They built ships, and when the time was right Aeneas led his fellow Trojans in search of a new home.

From Phrygia, Aeneas set sail with a fleet of twenty ships. He stopped at many islands, and on one a fortune-teller made a strange prediction. He told Aeneas he would be at home only when he was so hungry he ate the plate his food came on.

After a long voyage, Aeneas and his ships reached Sicily. But for old Anchises, the journey ended there. He died and was buried on the island. The final part of Aeneas's travels took him to Italy, where on the banks of the River Tiber he shared a meal with the rest of the Trojans. Such was their hunger that they ate the thin loaves of bread they were using as plates. The prediction had come true, and Aeneas knew he was home at last.

Aeneas was in the region known as Latium, the homeland of the Latins. He married the daughter of their king so that the Trojans and Latins were united as one people. Centuries later, when the city of Rome was founded in Latium, its citizens traced their family trees back to Aeneas the Trojan.

THE WOLF AND THE TWINS

Rome was a wonder to behold, the greatest city the world had ever known. A million people lived there – Romans, foreigners, and slaves. Within its walls were seven hills, the most important of which was the Palatine Hill. The Romans believed that this hill was where the city of Rome had begun.

A long time before Rome's first building stones were laid, there lived a cruel and unkind man called Amulius. His older brother, Numitor, was the king of a city in Latium. After a violent struggle, Amulius overthrew Numitor and made himself king. Then he turned on Numitor's family, killing his sons and forbidding his daughter, Rhea Silvia, from having children. Amulius did these terrible things to prevent Numitor from having descendants who might one day seek their revenge. Amulius was sure his plan would succeed. When Rhea Silvia gave birth to twin boys, whose father was the god Mars, Amulius ordered that they should be drowned in the River Tiber. His servants took the babies, whose names were Romulus and Remus, and placed them in a basket. But they were too kind-hearted to carry out Amulius's orders, and so they left the basket to float away to safety.

It came to rest beside a fig tree, where it was found by a she-wolf who had heard the babies' cries. She fed them with her own milk, and a woodpecker gave them scraps of food. When a shepherd saw this, he knew at once who the babies were. He took them home to his wife, and they raised them as their own sons.

Romulus and Remus grew into fine young men. One day, the shepherd met Numitor, and told him that his grandsons were alive and well. When Romulus and Remus learned who they really were, they sought revenge against Amulius. He was killed, and Numitor was king once more.

The brothers now decided to build a city of their own. They chose a place on the banks of the River Tiber, close to where they had been left to die as infants. But they quarreled as to who should name the city and become its king. Since they did not know which twin was the elder, they left it to the gods to send a sign. They stood on separate hills, and looked to the heavens. Remus saw six vultures, but Romulus saw twelve. Each believed the gods had meant him to be king – Remus because he saw the birds first, Romulus because he had seen the most.

A fight began, and Romulus killed his brother. By himself Romulus built the city on the hill which the Romans later called the Palatine Hill. He named the city Rome, after himself.

CLAUDIA AND THE GREAT MOTHER

In 204 BC Rome was at war with Carthage, a city on the north coast of Africa. The Carthaginian army had invaded Italy, and the Romans were desperate to find a way to drive the foreigners from their land.

Rome's leaders consulted the Sibylline Books – a collection of prophecies. They guided the Romans in times of trouble, and in the war with Carthage a prophecy told them how to defeat their enemy. It said: "The mother is absent. You must find her. When she comes, she must be received by honest hands."

The Romans were puzzled, and a group of them went to the oracle, or fortune-teller, at Delphi, in Greece, for more information. There they were told to: "Fetch the Great Mother who lives on Mount Ida." Now they knew what they must do to save Rome, for they knew that the Great Mother was none other than the goddess Cybele, the Mother of the Gods. Her symbol on Earth was a sacred stone, and just as the oracle had said, it was on Mount Ida, in the land of Phrygia. The Romans had to take the stone to Rome.

With the stone on board their ship, the Romans sailed back to Rome. But as their journey neared its end, disaster struck. As the ship entered the mouth of the River Tiber, it became stuck on a sandbank.

Strong men pulled on ropes tied to the ship, but it would not move. People grew worried that the goddess Cybele was unhappy. Perhaps this was an omen that Rome would lose the war. Then a woman called Claudia Quinta, who had been wrongly accused of a crime she had not committed, prayed to Cybele. With arms held high, Claudia prayed that Cybele would send a sign to prove she was innocent.

Then Claudia gently pulled on one of the ropes tied to the ship and, miraculously, it moved as easily as if it was a toy. This sign from heaven proved Claudia's innocence. Freed from the sandbank, the ship sailed into port.

Just as the prophecy had forecast, the Great Mother had been received by honest hands, and now that the sacred stone was in Rome, the Romans knew they would soon win the war.

THE SACRED FIRE OF ROME

Long before Rome became a great city, it was a small hill village. Inside each crudely built house was a hearth where a fire burned. There was no chimney, and smoke was left to find its way out through gaps in the walls and roof. Fires were kept permanently alight in people's homes as an act of worship to the gods: a cold hearth meant an empty, godless house. Rome's first fire, said the Romans, had been lit from a spark brought by Aeneas from the faraway city of Troy. Aeneas, the father of the Romans, had carried the sacred fire of Troy across seas and mountains, and it was his gift to the people of Rome.

As the years passed, the village grew. There were other villages on nearby hills, and they grew too, until eventually they came together to make a town. From that town came the city of Rome.

Rome was a magnificent city. At its center was the Forum, a large area filled with temples, arches, columns, and statues. From one of the temples a plume of smoke drifted into the sky. This was the Temple of Vesta, built in honor of the goddess of the hearth. It was a small temple and, unlike the others, it was round. It was built that way to remind Romans of the first houses and the city's humble beginnings.

A fire was kept constantly alight inside the Temple of Vesta, just like the fires that had burned inside Rome's first houses. It was the sacred fire of Rome. If it died, Rome would be in danger.

Near the temple was the House of Vesta. It was the home of six priestesses called Vestal Virgins. They became priestesses while still children, between the ages of six and ten, and then served the temple for thirty years. Their main duty was to keep the temple fire burning day and night, never letting it go out. But there were occasions when storms raged and drafts blew the fire out. When this happened, the Vestals were accused of neglecting their duties, and they were flogged. Some, however, escaped this punishment by performing miracles. Take, for example, the priestess Aemilia, who was accused of allowing the fire to die. As her accusers watched, she prayed to the goddess Vesta to send a sign to prove she was innocent of the crime. Aemilia ripped a piece of linen from her dress and threw it onto the fire's cold ashes. A wisp of gray smoke curled up from the cloth. Then, out of the smoke came fire. Rome's sacred fire burned bright once more, the city was safe, and Aemilia was spared from punishment.

THE SLAVE GIRLS SAVE THE CITY

In 390 BC Rome was looted by the Gauls, who came from uncivilized lands to the north. The Gauls stayed in Rome for many months, and only left after they were given a large amount of gold.

With the barbarians gone, the Romans expected life to return to normal. But they were mistaken. Rome had been weakened by the Gauls, and after they left a second attack was made against the city. This time,

Rome was attacked by the Latins – the people in whose territory Rome was built. The army of the Latins camped outside Rome, and ambassadors were sent into the city with a message. It said: "Send us your daughters to be our brides, for we wish the Latins and the Romans to be brought closer together." When the message was read out, there was panic in the streets, and for a while no one knew what to do. Then a slave girl, whose name was Philotis, came forward. She had an idea.

Philotis said she and other young slave girls should go to the Latins and pretend to be freeborn Roman women. Then, at night, she would signal to the Romans that they could attack their enemy while they lay in their beds. The Romans listened as Philotis explained her plan. All agreed it was their only hope to save Rome from disaster.

Philotis and her fellow slave girls were given fine clothes and gold jewelry to wear, and dressed as brides they went into the camp of the Latins. Once inside they told the Latins that it was a special day for the Romans too. They said it was a festival day, when Romans drank, ate, and enjoyed themselves. In the feast that followed, the slave girls served the Latins with food and drink. The Latins, who were soon drunk, fell into a deep sleep. While the girls hid the Latins' swords,

Philotis climbed a fig tree and waved a burning torch. This was the signal, and an army of Roman soldiers left Rome and headed toward the Latins' camp. Unseen, they crept into the camp and slaughtered the Latins as they slept.

Rome was safe, and every year thereafter, on July 7, a feast was held to honor Philotis and the other girls. Called the "Feast of the Fig Tree," it was a day when female servants were allowed to do as they pleased, and when Romans remembered how their city had been saved by the bravery of the slave girls.

77

THE BATTLE OF THE CHAMPIONS

In the early days of Rome, the nearby city of Alba Longa was its rival. It too wanted to be the region's leading city, and its people, the Albans, thought they should be the masters of Rome. But while the Romans and the Albans quarreled, they both knew their real enemy was across the River Tiber in Etruria. This was where the Etruscans lived, an old and powerful people who had lived in Italy far longer than either the Romans or the Albans.

The Roman and Alban leaders knew that if their armies fought each other, both sides would be weakened. It would leave them open to attack from the Etruscans, who would surely be the winners. And so the Romans and the Albans decided on a plan to settle their differences.

Each side chose a set of identical triplets to fight for them. The three Horatius brothers would fight for Rome, and the Curatius brothers would represent the Albans. It would be the Battle of the Champions, the fight to end all fights.

Clad in armor and brandishing swords, the Roman three attacked the Alban triplets. Before long, the Albans were wounded, and two of the Romans lay dead. The third, whose name was Publius Horatius, fled from the battlefield.

Onlookers watched as the three Albans chased Horatius. But Horatius was cunning. He was not running away out of fear, but because he knew the Albans were injured and their wounds would slow them down. Sure enough, the wounded Albans chased Horatius at different speeds, and he was able to turn and kill them one by one.

Horatius was declared the champion of champions, and Rome was proclaimed the supreme city. In recognition of his great deed, Horatius was awarded the cloaks and swords of the fallen Albans.

In Rome, Horatius was greeted as a hero. But when his sister met him she burst into tears. Only then did Horatius discover that she had been engaged to one of the Albans he had killed. Overcome with rage, Horatius plunged his sword into her heart crying: "So perish all Roman women who mourn a foe!"

By this terrible act, Horatius had taken the law into his own hands. He stood trial and was sentenced to death by hanging. But the Roman people could not bring themselves to execute their hero, and so Horatius, the man who had single-handedly defeated the Albans, was set free.

THE RAPE OF LUCRETIA

In the days when Rome was ruled by an unpopular family of kings called the Tarquins, the Romans were at war with the nearby city of Ardea. One day, during a long siege, a Roman general called Collatinus fell into conversation with other commanders. They talked about their wives at home in Rome, and which of them was leading the most virtuous life.

Collatinus said that his wife, Lucretia, would win the contest. The others disagreed, and to solve the argument they rode to Rome to visit their wives by surprise. This way they would discover who was leading the most virtuous life.

The men went to their homes at night. All of the women, except one, were enjoying themselves at elegant dinner parties. Their husbands were shocked. But when Collatinus visited Lucretia, he found her at work with her maid-servants, spinning wool. She alone had lived up to everything her husband had claimed for her.

But Lucretia was more than just well-behaved. Men were struck by her great beauty, and one, Sextus Tarquinius, who had ridden to Rome with her husband, fell in love with her. He was a Tarquin, son of the king. A few days later Tarquinius returned secretly to Lucretia's house, where he was greeted as an honored guest. He told Lucretia he had fallen in love with her. Lucretia would not hear of it. Tarquinius was determined to get his own way, and so he threatened to kill Lucretia and a slave. Lucretia was faced with a terrible choice: whether to give in to Tarquinius or die. Either way, her fate was sealed, and she gave in to the vile demands of Tarquinius.

After Tarquinius had left, Lucretia summoned her father and her husband. Each brought a friend. The four men listened to Lucretia's story. They did their best to comfort her, saying she should not feel guilty since it was Tarquinius who had forced himself upon her. Lucretia felt her honor had been taken from her. She picked up a knife and stabbed herself through the heart. As for Tarquinius, he did not get away with his crime. When the people heard what he had done they rose up against the Tarquins and overthrew the monarchy. From then on Rome was a republic, no longer ruled by kings, but by men chosen by the people. For this, Lucretia was forever remembered as the woman who gave the Romans their freedom from tyrants.

QUEEN DIDO TRIES TO TRAP AENEAS

Many tales are told about Aeneas and the adventures he had as he sailed from Troy to Italy. Before Aeneas reached Italy, his ships were blown off course by a storm. Many of his faithful sailors were feared drowned. His seven remaining ships, their sails torn and timbers battered, headed to the shelter of an unfamiliar coastline. The coastline was that of north Africa, and Aeneas landed close to the city of Carthage, the home of Queen Dido. Aeneas ordered his crew to stay by their ships and set off toward the city. As he walked through the country, the goddess Venus appeared and told him about the people he would meet. To protect him, the goddess shrouded Aeneas in a mist which made him invisible.

Inside the city's great temple he watched as Queen Dido commanded her people to do her work. And then he saw something which amazed him, for standing in a group were the Trojan sailors he thought had drowned at sea. This was powerful magic indeed, and Queen Dido must surely be a great ruler to pluck men from the teeth of a storm. She listened as the Trojans told of their adventures with Aeneas, and how it was

his plan to build a new city to replace Troy.

When Queen Dido said she must find Aeneas, the mist of invisibility that hid the hero from view suddenly lifted. Aeneas was revealed!

That night, at a banquet, Aeneas entertained the queen. She was captivated, not only by the stories she heard, but by Aeneas himself. She was soon in love with him, and began to plan a way of keeping him for herself.

But the gods had other plans for Aeneas, for they knew it was his destiny to sail to Italy. They watched as Queen Dido plotted to marry Aeneas and trap him in Carthage. Aeneas seemed unable to break free from her spell. The gods knew that they must act, and they sent Mercury with a message.

Mercury, the god of travelers and messages, told Aeneas that his future lay in Italy, not with Queen Dido. When Aeneas, who was now free of her magic, told her he was leaving, she pleaded with him to stay. But it was no use. Aeneas knew he must continue on his journey.

Overcome with grief, Queen Dido

ordered a fire to be built. She wanted to destroy everything that reminded her of Aeneas. Then, as she watched the Trojans' ships depart, she fell on a sword and died. The fire was lit, and its flames consumed more than just the memories of Aeneas, for it was now Queen Dido's funeral pyre.

As for Aeneas, he never looked back. He sailed to Italy and his future as the father of the Roman people.

CASTOR AND POLLUX – THE HEAVENLY TWINS

To the east of Italy is the land of Greece. The Greeks were very wise, and the Romans learned many things from them. When the Romans learned about Zeus and the other gods of the Greeks, they began to worship them as their own. The Romans gave them new names, which is how the Greek god Zeus became the Roman god Jupiter.

The Greeks told stories about their gods. One story was about "Zeus's boys" who were twin brothers called Castor and Polydeuces. The Romans called them Castor and Pollux, and, as time passed, they made up their own stories about the "heavenly twins."

The Romans told how Castor and Pollux helped them win a battle against their neighbors, the Latins. Out of nowhere rode the twins. On white stallions at the head of the Roman cavalry, they charged at the Latins, who were soon defeated. Then, by some strange magic, the twins appeared in the center of Rome, many miles from the battlefield. They watered their horses in a sacred pool, told the crowds about the Roman victory over the Latins, and vanished.

In another story told by the Romans, Castor and Pollux were seen by a man called Publius Vatinius. He was on his way to Rome when he had a vision. It was late at night, and out of the darkness came the heavenly twins, riding along the road.

Their sudden appearance startled Vatinius. But he had nothing to fear, for the twins had good news, saying the Roman army had been victorious against their enemies, the Macedonians.

Vatinius hurried on to Rome and gave the news to the city's leaders. They did not believe him. They thought he was tricking them with lies – why would Castor and Pollux come to Vatinius and not them? Poor old Vatinius was taken away and locked up.

Many weeks later a messenger brought news that the Roman army really had defeated the Macedonians. At once, the people knew that Vatinius had told the truth – Castor and Pollux really had come to him, just as he had said.

Vatinius was set free, and to make amends for the way he had been wronged he was given some land. As for Castor and Pollux, they continued to be worshiped by the Romans, in the temple built in their honor.

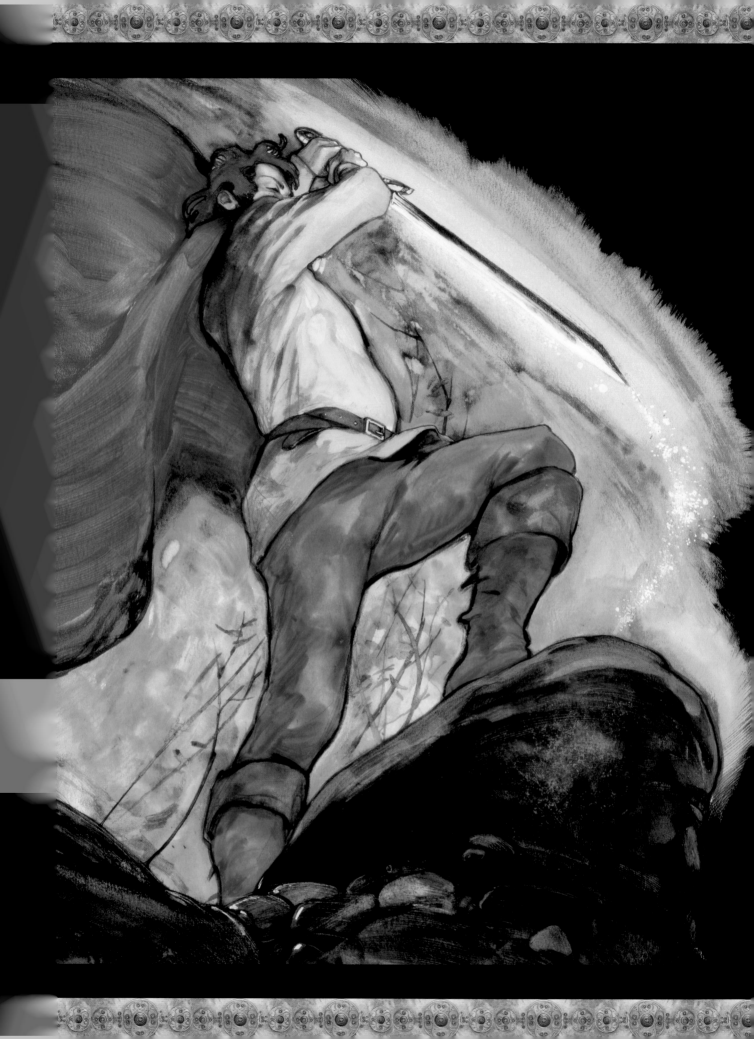

CELTS

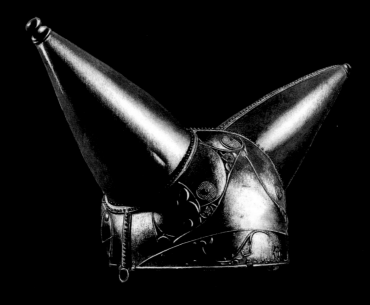

INTRODUCTION

The long history of the Celtic world has not come down to us in texts written by the Celts themselves. Instead, scholars have patched together the rather biased records left to us by their enemies, the Greeks and Romans, with the painstaking work of archeologists, to create a picture of one of the greatest of the early European peoples. Celtic tribes occupied much of continental Europe and the British Isles until the 1st century BC, when the Romans conquered almost all their lands. They left a rich store of burials, objects from everyday life, and works of art to intrigue future generations. We have also inherited many versions of their myths, initially preserved by Christian monks and then rewritten in medieval times. In this chapter we retell myths from different times and places in the ancient Celtic world.

HOW THE CELTS CAME TO IRELAND

The Irish myths tell of five invasions of Ireland before the Celts. The first was led by Cessair, daughter of Noah's son, Bith. They arrived forty days before the Flood in which all but one of them drowned. The survivor was Fintan mac Bochra, who lived for 5,500 years, disguised as a salmon, an eagle, and a hawk, and saw all that followed.

The next invasion took place 300 years later and was led by Parthalon, who was descended from Noah's son, Japheth. In Ireland, however, Parthalon's people often had to fight their enemies, the Fomorians.

They were descended from Noah's son, Ham, and were fierce and monstrous beings, with only one arm and one leg each. But, before they could defeat the Fomorians, Parthalon, and all but one of his people died of plague.

Thirty years after Parthalon's invasion, Ireland was invaded again, this time by Nemedh and his followers. Their descendants attacked the Fomorians but were unsuccessful. Only thirty of them survived and they fled to Britain, the Northern Isles, and Greece. Their descendants led the next two invasions. The first to arrive were the Fir Bholg from Greece.

They ruled Ireland for 37 years and divided it into the provinces of Ulster, Leinster, Connacht, Munster, and Meath. The Tuatha De Danann, descendants of the people who fled to the Northern Isles, then invaded and defeated the Fir Bholg at the First Battle of Magh Tuiredh. In this battle, however, Nuadhu, the leader of the Tuatha De Danann, lost his right arm. This meant that he could no longer rule and his place was taken by Bres.

But Bres was a bad king and was forced to give up his throne. In revenge, he asked the Fomorians to gather an army. Meanwhile, the court physician made a silver arm for Nuadhu and he became king again. But his rule was brief – during a feast at Tara, he abdicated in favor of Lugh, a young warrior. Lugh led the Tuatha De Danann to victory against Bres at the Second Battle of Magh Tuiredh and drove the Fomorians into the sea.

After these five invasions, the Celts arrived. They landed in south-west Ireland and quickly defeated the Tuatha De Danann. Then they marched on Tara and defeated the Tuatha de Danann again, this time forcing them into exile.

TALES FROM THE OTHERWORLD

The Celts believed there was another world beneath the one they lived in. Reached through underground caves and hollows in the hills, it was known as the Otherworld. It was inhabited by spirits and magical beings, as well as some of their gods and goddesses, and was also where people went to live after they had died in the human world. But this new life did not last for ever, as people could also die in the Otherworld. When this happened, they returned to the human world as babies and started life all over again.

However, it was not always necessary to die to pass from the human world to the Otherworld or back again. At certain times of the year it was possible to go from one to the other. The best time to do this was at the great festival of Samhain, which took place on 1 November and marked the start of winter and the Celtic new year. The night before Samhain was thought to belong neither to the old year nor to the new, and great armies of spirits from the Otherworld chose this time to visit the human world. They came in peace and often joined in the human celebrations.

Sometimes individuals came from the Otherworld to bestow a gift on a human, but this could not be used for personal gain. Instead, it had to be used to help other people. One such gift was given to Rhiwallon, the first doctor in the Welsh family known as the Physicians of Myddfai, when he was visited by the Lady of the Lake. She gave him a bag of herbs and recipes, and showed him a secret place where the herbs he would need for his medicines grew. She also gave him the gift of healing, which he was able to pass on to his sons.

On other occasions, humans were taken into the Otherworld to receive their gift. This happened to the piper of Dunmore in Galway, who, no matter how he tried, could only play one tune on his pipes. He played it one night as he was crossing over a bridge and the sound attracted an animal spirit, called the Puca na Samhna. This spirit grabbed hold of the piper and, carrying him on his back, took him to a great feast being held in the Otherworld. The piper was asked to provide the music for the evening's entertainment and easily played many different tunes. As a reward, he was given money and a new set of pipes, before being carried back to the bridge to continue his journey home. When he got there, he remembered the skills he had learnt in the Otherworld and from then onward he was the best piper in Ireland.

THE LEGEND OF MAON

Maon was the great-grandson of the legendary Ugainy the Great, who ruled over the whole of Ireland and a large part of Western Europe. With his Gaulish wife, Kesair, Ugainy had two sons, Laery and Covac. When Laery inherited the kingdom after Ugainy's death, Covac was so filled with jealousy that he became ill. He knew that the only way he could take the kingdom from Laery was by killing him, but whenever Covac met Laery, Laery always had an armed escort with him.

Finally a Druid advised Covac to pretend that he had died and send a message to Laery, inviting him to the burial. Covac did this, and when Laery and his son Ailill came to see the body, Covac quickly jumped up and stabbed them both to death.

Covac's illness then left him, but he could not forget the jealousy he had felt toward his brother. So, as a final revenge, he took Ailill's young son, Maon, and made him eat a part of Laery's heart and a part of Ailill's heart, before forcing him

to swallow a mouse and her babies. This upset Maon so much that he could no longer speak and, realizing that the child was no longer a threat to him, Covac sent him away to live with the ruler of Feramorc and his daughter Moriath.

From Feramorc Maon went to Gaul to live with his great-grandmother's people and there he grew into a fine young man.

Meanwhile Moriath, who had fallen in love with him, did not forget the handsome young Maon. She was determined that he would come back to Ireland and regain his kingdom.

She wrote a love song for him and sent her father's harpist to sing it to him. Maon was so moved that his speech returned and, with the help of his grandmother's people, he raised an army and sailed to Ireland to find Covac. After a long search he found his old enemy and forced him to fight for the kingdom.

The battle took place at Dinrigh and Maon was victorious, killing Covac along with many of his nobles and warriors. Having reclaimed his kingdom, Maon married Moriath, the woman whose love had helped to make his victory possible.

THE TRAGEDY OF CUCHULAIN

When Cuchulain, the great hero of Ulster, was a young man, he fell in love with a beautiful woman called Emer. She refused to marry him until he proved himself in battle.

Determined to do this, Cuchulain traveled to the Land of Shadows where the fierce and mighty she-warrior, Skatha, lived. He asked her to teach him her skills and she agreed. While he was there, Skatha declared war on Aoife, the most powerful she-warrior in the world.

When their armies met, Cuchulain and two of Skatha's sons killed six of Aoife's best warriors. But Aoife knew that she was stronger than Skatha and so she challenged her to fight in single combat. Then Cuchulain offered to fight in Skatha's place and, defeating Aoife by trickery, he threw her over his shoulder and carried her back to Skatha's camp. The two women soon made peace, and Cuchulain and Aoife became friends and then lovers. But Cuchulain could only stay in the Land of Shadows for a year and a day and, by the time he had to leave, Aoife was expecting his child. Cuchulain gave her a gold ring and told her that, if the child were a boy, she was to call him Connla and give him the ring when he was big enough and then send him in search of his father.

Aoife agreed to this, but after Connla was born she heard that Cuchulain had married Emer. Overcome by jealousy, she decided to have her revenge. When the time came for Connla to go in search of his father, she made him promise not to tell anyone his name, not to turn his back, and never to refuse a challenge.

All went well until he reached Ulster where King Conor and his noblemen were gathered on the beach. Looking out to sea, they saw a boat with golden oars approaching. Not knowing the young man in it, Conor told him to turn back, but he refused to do so. Conor then sent his fiercest warriors to challenge him, but he defeated them one by one.

Finally Conor sent Cuchulain to fight the stranger. The fight was long and at one point Cuchulain almost drowned. Then he remembered the Gae Bholg, a special weapon that Skatha had given him. He quickly threw it and the stranger fell, fatally wounded. As Cuchulain pulled him from the water, he saw the ring on the young man's finger and realized that he had just killed Connla, his only son.

THE DAGDA'S PORRIDGE BOWL

The Dagda was one of the great chieftains of the legendary Tuatha De Danann. He was also the most important god of the Celts in Ireland. His name means the "good god," but he was also known as the "father of all" and "lord of perfect knowledge." His possessions included a cauldron that never ran out of food, and a magic pig that could be killed and eaten, then come alive again ready to be killed and eaten again the next day. He also had a magic club – with one end he could kill nine men with a single blow, and with a touch of the other end he could restore them to life.

As well as being the god of wisdom, the Dagda was also the god of the earth and enjoyed earthly pleasures. He was fond of music and played his harp to bring about the change in the seasons. He also enjoyed feasting and being in the company of beautiful women. The Dagda's enemies, the Fomorians, used this knowledge to try to prevent him from fighting against them in the Second Battle of Magh Tuiredh.

During a truce in the battle, the Fomorians found the Dagda resting and began mocking him over his great appetite. They challenged him to eat a meal of porridge, his favorite food, which they would cook for him. The Dagda accepted the challenge, and the preparations started.

As the Fomorians did not have a big enough cooking pot, they dug a hole in the ground and poured into it 80 cauldrons full of fresh milk, 80 cauldrons of oats, and 80 cauldrons of fat. To this they added whole sheep, pigs, and goats. The porridge was then boiled, and when it was ready, the Fomorians gave the Dagda an enormous spoon and told him to eat every scrap or be killed.

To their amazement, the Dagda did just this and, to make sure nothing was left behind, he used his finger to scrape the last drops out of the hole. After such a big meal, the Fomorians expected the Dagda to fall asleep and miss the rest of the battle, but instead he stayed wide awake.

Then the Fomorians remembered his love of beautiful women. They brought him a lovely young woman and left her in his company. They thought this would exhaust him, but once more they were wrong. The Dagda was soon revitalized and ready to return to battle. The young woman was so pleased with him that she took his side and helped him to defeat the Fomorians.

THE TALE OF PEREDUR

Peredur, a seventh son, was marked out by destiny for strange and high fortunes. His father and six brothers had all been slain in war, so his mother brought him up in a forest where he could learn nothing of warfare. But one evening Peredur saw three knights from Arthur's court in the forest. Entranced by the sight, he asked his mother who the men were. "They are angels, my son," she said. "Then I will go and become an angel with them," he replied. Peredur's mother could not discourage him, so in the end she gave him her blessing and told him to seek the Court of Arthur, where lived the best and boldest of knights.

Peredur set out on a bony piebald work horse, his only weapons a handful of sharp-pointed stakes. When he arrived at Arthur's castle he was rudely repulsed by the steward, Kai, for his rustic appearance. To win entrance, Peredur had to fight a ruffian knight who had offended the court. Peredur beat the knight and took his armor, weapons, and horse.

Setting out on his own, he came to a castle by a lake. Peredur entered the castle where he was received by a very old man. After eating, the man said "I am your uncle, your mother's brother." When he left, the old man warned him never to ask the meaning of whatever might puzzle him if no one saw fit to explain it to him.

Peredur rode until he came to the Castle of Wonders. He entered the great hall and was received by the lord. After dining, the lord asked Peredur if he knew how to use a sword. "If I were to receive instruction," said Peredur, "I think I could." The lord gave Perdur a sword and told him to strike an iron staple in the floor. Peredur did so and cut the staple in two. But the sword also flew into two parts. "Put the two parts together," said the lord. Peredur did so and they were one again. A second time this was done with the same result. The third time neither the sword nor the staple would reunite. "Your have reached two-thirds of your strength," said the lord. Then he too declared that he was Peredur's uncle. As they spoke, two youths entered the hall carrying a lance dripping with blood. Next came two maidens carrying a glowing silver dish on which lay a man's severed head. The whole party began to wail and lament. Peredur did not ask for an explanation, but went to bed.

Later he learnt that the head in the silver dish belonged to a cousin and the lance was the weapon used to slay him. Peredur had been shown these things so that he would avenge them. The evil had been done to Peredur's family by the nine sorceresses of Gloucester. With Arthur's help, Peredur slew all nine and vengeance was accomplished.

HOW CUCHULAIN GOT HIS NAME

The smith was a very important person in Celtic society. Everyone depended on his skills for the tools and weapons they needed to survive. Most smiths worked in small communities, making simple objects for everyday use. However, the best of them worked at court, making weapons and beautiful objects in silver and gold for the king and his closest companions.

One of the most famous smiths was Culann, who worked at the court of King Conchobar. Culann was so rich that he could afford to give a feast splendid enough to invite the king himself. At that time the king was looking after his foster son, Sedanta, who was seven years old, and so he invited the boy to go with him to the feast. Sedanta was busy playing with his friends, however, and so he told the king he would follow him to Culann's house when he had finished his game.

By the time the king and his courtiers reached Culann's house, dusk was falling, and as Culann invited them in and the feast began, Sedanta was quite forgotten. The gates to the house were securely barred and Culann let his favorite hound loose in the grounds to protect his property and his guests from would-be robbers and other wrongdoers.

All went well until halfway through the evening. Suddenly the mighty barking of the hound was heard above the sound of merrymaking, warning Culann that a stranger was approaching his house. As his guests fell quiet and listened, the barking changed to howling and then to silence.

Puzzled by this, Culann and his guests ran out to see what had happened. They found Sedanta at the gate with the hound lying dead at his feet; he had killed it with his bare hands after it had attacked him. Culann's guests praised Sedanta for his bravery, but Culann himself was sad over the death of his favorite hound, which had only been trying to protect him.

Seeing the smith's sorrow, Sedanta asked to be given a puppy from the same strain as the hound and promised he would train it himself until it was as good as the dog he had killed. When Culann agreed to this, Sedanta made him another promise. Asking for a shield and a spear, he said he would guard Culann as well as any dog until the puppy was completely trained. Culann accepted the offer and from that day onward Sedanta became known as Cuchulain, which means "the hound of Culann."

THE SWORD IN THE STONE

The legends of King Arthur tell us that after the death of Uther Pendragon there was no king in England. Though Uther Pendragon had had a son, he was only a baby when his father died and Merlin the Magician had spirited him away to a foster home until the time was right for him to reveal himself as the true king. The country fell into chaos as the nobles fought each other for the title and there was no one to enforce the laws of the land. Things went from bad to worse, then Merlin came up with an idea.

He produced a huge stone, in which was a sword. Gold letters around the stone said that whoever could pull out the sword was the true king by right of birth. Many tried, but no one could move the sword. Finally it was decided that every noble in the land should be given a chance to remove the sword and a date was set for them all to compete.

Among the nobles who went on that day was Ector, with his son Kay and foster son Arthur. When they arrived, however, Kay realized that he had left his own sword at home and asked Arthur to go and fetch it for him. Arthur went, but when he got to the house, the door was locked. Not wanting to let his foster

brother down, Arthur remembered the sword in the stone and decided to take that for Kay instead.

Arthur pulled it out easily, but Kay recognized the sword and took it to show his father. Ector called for Arthur and asked him if any one had seen him remove it. Arthur replied that he had been alone at the time and so Ector told him to go back to the stone and replace the sword. When Arthur had done this, Ector then tried to pull the sword out himself, but he could not move it. Kay also tried, but without success. Arthur then tried again and once more pulled it out with no effort.

Ector realized that his foster son must really be the son of Uther Pendragon, though he knew it would be difficult to persuade the other noblemen to accept this and allow Arthur to rule over them.

Three more competitions were organized and at each one Arthur was the only person who could pull the sword from the stone. The noblemen would still not accept him, however, and so a fourth competition was held and this time the common people were also invited. When they saw Arthur pull the sword from the stone, they at once accepted him as king and he was crowned the very same day.

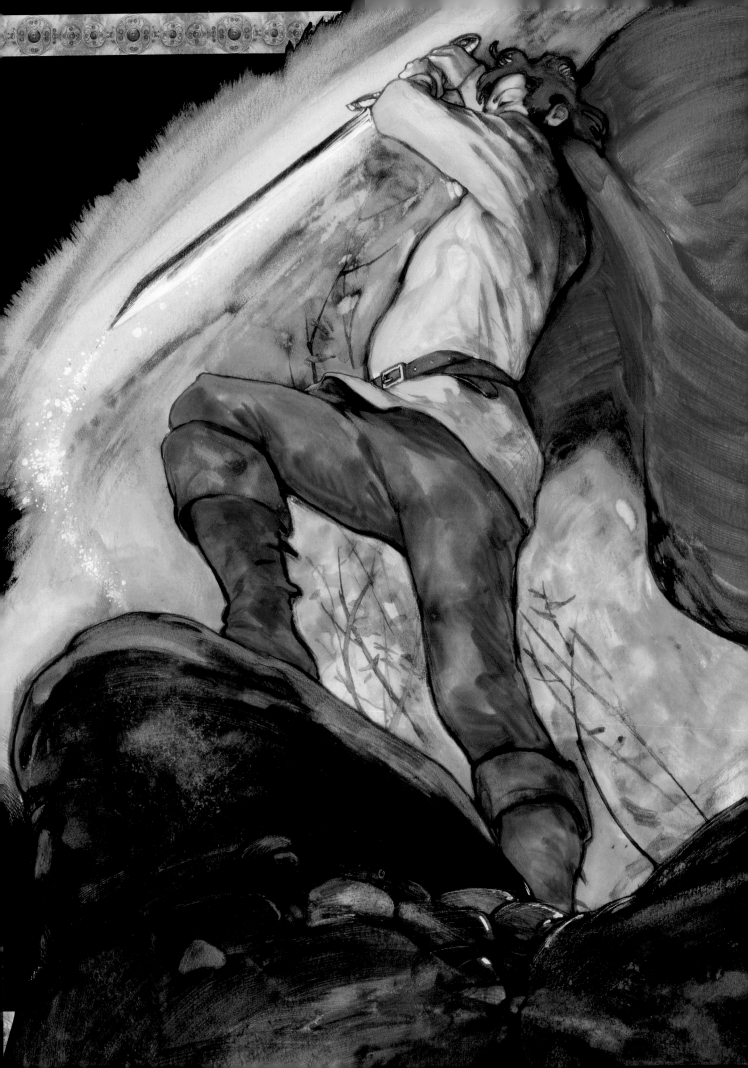

THE CHILDREN OF LIR

Lir was a chieftain of the Tuatha De Danaan who lived at Finaghy in the north of Ireland. When his wife died, his ruler, Bov Dearg, invited Lir to his court and suggested he marry one of his three foster-daughters. Lir agreed and chose Eve, the eldest of the three. They went back to Finaghy where, after a year of marriage, Eve gave birth to twins, Fionnuala and Aedh, a girl and a boy. A year later, Eve gave birth to twin sons, Fiachra and Conn, but she died in childbirth.

Lir was heartbroken and only the love of his four children kept him alive. Then Bov Dearg invited Lir again and suggested that he marry Eve's sister, Aoife. Lir agreed and at first things went well. Aoife loved the children and they loved her. But gradually she came to think that Lir loved his children more than he loved her.

One day Aoife took the children to visit Bov Dearg. Three times on the journey Aoife stopped her chariot and told her servants to kill the children, but they refused. On the shores of Lough Derravaragh she stopped again and told the children to go and bathe in the lake. As they did so she cast a spell, turning them into swans but leaving them their human voices.

When Fionnuala asked how long the spell would last, Aoife realized what a terrible thing she had done. The children would spend 300 years on Lough Derravaragh, 300 years on the wild Sea of Moyle, and then 300 years on lonely Inish Gluaire, before regaining their human bodies – when the sound of a bell would start to change Ireland.

The children bore their punishment bravely. For the first 300 years they had many visitors who brought them news of their friends and family and listened to their sweet singing. On the Sea of Moyle the visitors were fewer, and on Inish Gluaire they saw no one at all.

Finally the day came for the spell to end and, still in the shape of swans, they flew back to their home. As they landed, a Christian monk rang a bell, inviting people to join the new Christian religion and pray. As Aoife promised, this broke the spell, but when Lir's children changed back to their human forms, they were no longer young. Instead they were more than 900 years old and everything they had known and loved when they were human before had gone. All that remained was their love for each other, and as the saint blessed them, they linked arms and died.

VIKINGS

INTRODUCTION

The Vikings burst onto the stage of European history at the end of the 8th century with the first of a series of devastating raids on Britain and continental Europe. Lasting around 300 years (AD 800–1100), the Viking Age was spectacular and had enormous impact. The Vikings were a restless and daring people; from their rugged homelands in Norway, Denmark, and Sweden, they explored Europe, setting up trade links with the Asian, Arab, and North African peoples on its eastern and southern fringes. They also traveled west, raiding and settling in England, Iceland, Greenland, and even North America, a good 500 years before Columbus! The Viking Age had faded by the 13th century, as the coming of Christianity changed Scandinavian society, but its rich heritage continues to the present day.

THE BIRTH OF THE WORLD

The Vikings believed that the earth was created out of a great empty space called Ginnungagap. To the north of Ginnungagap lay the icy realm of Niflheim, while to the south was Muspell, which was made from flames and fire. Then Ginnungagap was slowly filled with ice from Niflheim. As the ice got nearer to Muspell it began to melt and two creatures were formed out of it. One was Ymir, the first Frost Giant, and the other was Audumla, a giant cow. She lived by licking the ice and Ymir fed on her milk. While Ymir lay sleeping, more Frost Giants and Giantesses grew out of his sweat.

One day Audumla found a huge, humanlike figure when she was licking the ice. She freed it from the ice and it turned into Buri. He later had a son called Bor. In his turn, Bor had three sons who became the first gods. Their names were Odin, Vili and Ve. The gods hated the Frost Giants because they were harsh and cruel. They killed Ymir and made the world out of his body, using his flesh for the earth and his bones and teeth for the mountains and rocks. His blood was used for the seas and rivers and his skull was made into the dome of the sky, while his brain became the clouds. Bright sparks of fire from Muspell were then tossed into the sky to make the sun and moon, and the stars and planets.

After this, Odin, Vili, and Ve shaped the first humans from the roots of an ash tree and an elm tree which they found on the seashore. They called the man Ask because he was made from the ash tree, while the woman was called Embla because she was made from the elm. The gods breathed life into Ask and Embla and they became the ancestors of all humans. Around the same time, Odin, Vili and Ve made the dwarfs from maggots that had crawled out of Ymir's flesh and gave four of them the task of holding up the sky.

Nothing more is heard of Vili and Ve, but Odin became the most important of all the gods and goddesses. From his home in Asgard he could see into the future and knew what fate held in store for everyone. He also knew everything that happened in the Nine Realms which made up the world and often traveled in disguise from one realm to another.

HEIMDALL AND HUMAN SOCIETY

One day Heimdall decided to visit Midgard. Disguised as a man and calling himself Rig, he first went to the home of a poor man and his wife. Their names were Ai and Edda and their tiny house was built from blocks of turf. However, when Rig knocked on the door and asked for food and shelter, they welcomed him in and shared their coarse bread and simple stew with him. Rig stayed with Ai and Edda for three nights and repaid their kindness by causing the childless Edda to have a son. He was named Thrall, meaning slave, and in due course he married a woman called Bondmaid and they became the ancestors of all future thralls.

Rig went next to a prosperous-looking farm, owned by Alf and his childless wife, Amma. When he asked them for food and shelter, they also welcomed him in and fed him on calf-stew and other tasty foods. Again he stayed for three nights and repaid their kindness by causing Amma to have a son. This son was called Karl, meaning freeman. In due course he also married and had children. He and his wife became the ancestors of all future karls.

Finally Rig went to a great hall where wealthy Fathir and his childless wife, Mothir, lived. Again Rig asked for food and shelter and here he was entertained with the very best of everything. He stayed for three nights and repaid Fathir and Mothir's kindness by causing her to have a son too. His name was Jarl, meaning earl, and he grew up to be a wealthy nobleman and the ancestor of all future jarls.

With the three classes of Viking society thus created, Rig took on the form of Heimdall once more and went back to where he came from where he continued to guard the other gods and goddesses from their enemies.

The Vikings believed that there were nine different realms, arranged on three levels. At the top were Asgard and Vanaheim, homes of the gods and goddesses, and Alheim, home of the helpful Light Elves. In the middle came Midgard where humans lived, Utgard, home of the Giants, Nidavellir, home of the Dwarfs, and Svartalfheim, home of the mischevious Dark Elves. At the bottom were the miserable worlds of Niflheim and Muspell. The Nine Realms were held in place by the roots of the giant ash tree, Yggdrasil. Asgard and Midgard were also joined by a narrow bridge, called Bifrost. It was guarded by Heimdall, one of the Vanir gods.

THOR AND JORMUNGAND

Thor, god of Thunder, had vowed to slay the hideous serpent Jormungand. During one of his many voyages he was staying with the giant Hymir. One morning, as Hymir prepared his tackle for the day's fishing, Thor asked to go out to sea with him. Hymir agreed, and Thor rowed out vigorously to where the giant usually fished. Hymir asked Thor to stop, but the god kept rowing. He took them to where the serpent Jormungand lay with its awful coils twisted about the earth.

Thor baited his hook with a bull's head and cast it far out over the waters. The serpent appeared almost immediately, took the gruesome bait in its mouth and swallowed it greedily. When it felt the hook pricking its throat it began to thrash about wildly. It tugged so fiercely that Thor's fists were smashed against the boat's gunwhales. Thor strained   so hard against the line that the bottom of the boat gave way beneath him and his feet plunged down until they lodged in the seabed. With his boots thus firmly grounded, he began to haul the serpent towards the boat. He fixed the crazed animal with such a look as would freeze a mortal's blood, while the serpent's fiery gaze spat

poisoned arrows back at him. Just as Thor reached for his mighty hammer to deliver the fatal blow, the terrified Hymir bent forward and quickly cut the line with his fishing knife.

The monster fell back into the sea and vanished into the blue depths. Disgusted by his companion's cowardice, Thor dealt him a fierce blow with his hammer and then set off towards the shore, striding across the bottom of the sea.

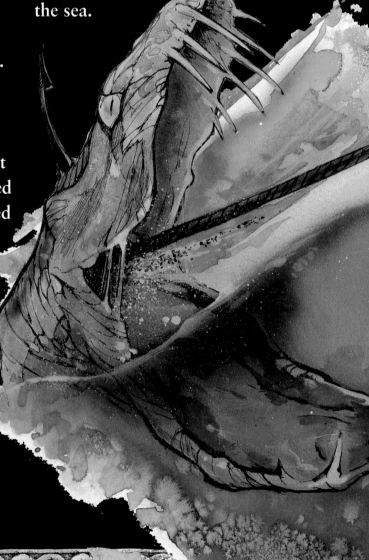

Thor and Jormungand would meet
again, during the Twilight of the Gods.
On that occasion Thor would succeed in
defeating his enemy, although it would
cost him his life.

Freyja and the dwarfs

Freyja was the Viking goddess of love and beauty. She had been married to Odin and, when he left her and disappeared without a trace, she wept tears of gold. She was very beautiful, however, and both men and gods wanted to marry her. She granted her favors to many and brought good harvests and healthy babies to the Viking farmers and their wives. Some of the Dwarfs and Giants also wanted to marry her, but Freyja thought they were not worthy of her attention.

As well as being beautiful herself, Freyja liked beautiful objects, especially jewelry, and this sometimes led her into trouble. Her worst problems came when she wanted a wonderful gold necklace called Brisingamen. It had been made by the Dwarfs, who were skilled metalworkers but were also very cunning. She tried to buy it from them, but the price they asked was that she must spend a night each with four of them in turn. Freyja wanted Brisingamen so much that she agreed to do this.

When the mischievous Loki found out, he told Odin who commanded him to take Brisingamen from Freyja as a punishment for what she had done. Knowing that Freyja liked Brisingamen so much that she even wore it when she was asleep, Loki changed himself into a fly and flew into her bedchamber. He then changed into a flea and bit her on the cheek. This made her turn over in her sleep and Loki was able to unfasten the clasp which held Brisingamen and steal the necklace from around her neck without waking her.

When Freyja realized Brisingamen was missing, she guessed Odin was involved and went to him to demand its return. He agreed to give it back to her, but in return she had to cause wars between kings on earth. She also had to become a goddess of death, choosing half of the bravest warriors as she flew over the battlefields in her chariot which was pulled by two cats.

AEGIR'S FEAST

Loki lived in Asgard and was treated as one of the gods, even though he was the son of two Fire Giants. In his youth, he loved adventures, mystery and disguise. He also amused the gods with his mischief and trickery. Sometimes he was deceitful, however, and told lies about other people to get them into trouble. Eventually the gods began to tire of his behavior and wanted little to do with him. This made Loki very bitter and instead of being mischievous, he became spiteful and evil.

In this new mood Loki grew jealous of Balder. He was Odin's son and was loved by everyone for his kindness and his wisdom. He lived happily with his wife, Nanna, and brought peace and harmony wherever he went. But Loki used trickery to kill Balder, then prevented him from returning to

life by refusing to weep for him. The gods were heartbroken over Balder's death. Their mourning lasted for a very long time, during which Loki avoided their company. Then Aegir, the sea god, and his wife, Ran, decided everyone had been sad for long enough. They organized a great feast in their underwater hall and invited all the gods and goddesses to it to cheer them up. Loki was the only one not to be invited, but he was determined to go.

Using trickery again, he appeared in Aegir's hall when the feast was well under way and the gods had started to be happy again.

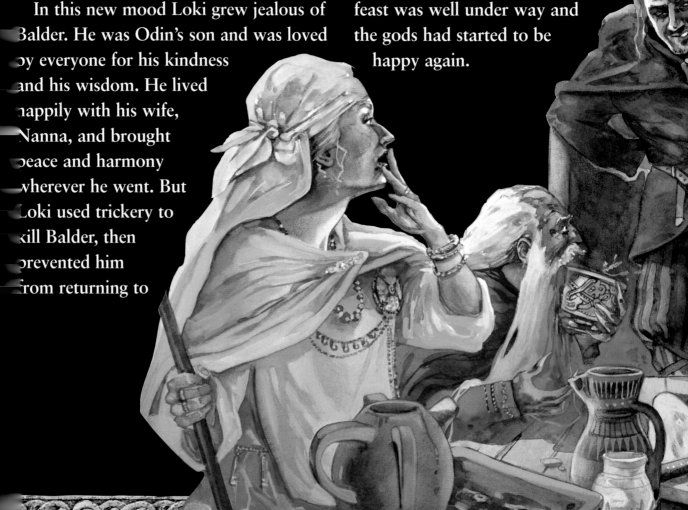

This angered Loki so much that he made a speech insulting each of them and telling all their secrets. He then tried to flee from the hall, but the gods chased after him. To get away, he disguised himself as a salmon and leapt into a waterfall. He could no longer fool the gods, however, and they quickly got a net to catch him. They decided he should suffer for what he had done and so they took him to a cave in the mountains and tied him across sharp rocks. Then they placed a poisonous snake above his head so that venom from its fangs would drip onto his face and cause him great pain. Only his wife felt sorry for him and she held a bowl to catch the poison. But whenever she had to empty it, the poison fell on Loki's face again and he would writhe in agony until she returned.

THE VALKYRIES

Asgard, the home of the Aesir gods, was divided into many different halls. The most magnificent was Valhalla, which belonged to Odin. Its roof was made from golden spears and its walls were lined with golden shields. The name meant the Hall of the Slain and it was the final home of Viking warriors and kings who had been killed in battle. Half of these warriors were chosen by the goddess Freyja. The rest were chosen by the Valkyries, Odin's maidservants who sometimes dressed like warriors themselves. They had names such as Battle, Shrieking and Shaker and often swooped over a battle on their horses to direct the fighting and make sure that the warriors they had chosen were killed.

Once the warriors were dead, the Valkyries picked them up and transported them to Valhalla. They usually went one by one on horseback, but if the Valkyries had chosen a lot of warriors or the battle had been near the sea, they could go by boat instead. As they reached Valhalla, other Valkyries came out to meet them, carrying golden drinking horns filled with mead or beer. The warriors were restored to life and their wounds were swiftly healed as they were welcomed into Odin's hall. There a great feast of roast boar was set out for them and they could sit at the table and eat their fill, waited on by the Valkyries and surrounded by the other warriors who had died before them. They told tales of their adventures and of the battles they had been in. And, as the night went on, they laughed and sang and got happily drunk, before going to their beds to sleep.

When they woke next morning, they were refreshed and ready for battle again. They put on their helmets and picked up their swords, spears, battle-axes and shields. Then they went to a special battleground where they could fight against each other all day. They could be wounded or even killed there, but in the evening they all returned to Valhalla where the wounded were healed and the dead restored to life once more. The Valkyries had another great feast waiting for them in the hall and once more the warriors ate and drank, told tales, laughed and sang throughout the evening. Then they went to bed and rested, ready for the daily round of fighting and feasting to begin again.

THE VANIR GODS

The gods of the Vanir family were the guardians of pastures and forests, rain and sunlight. They brought peace and good harvests to the land and controlled storms at sea. Originally they had all lived in Vanaheim and had been enemies of the Aesir gods. When the two families made peace with each other the three most important Vanir gods went to live in Asgard. They were Njord, the main sea god, and his children Frey and Freyja. Njord's wife was a Mountain Giantess called Skadi. But their marriage was unhappy because she loved the mountains and Njord loved the sea. Eventually they agreed to live apart and their children lived with Njord.

In spite of his father's unhappy experience, Frey also wanted to marry a Giantess whose name was Gerd. He had spied her one day when he had broken the rules of Asgard by sneaking into Odin's hall and sitting on Odin's throne. From there he could see into Jotunheim, the land of the Frost Giants, where the beautiful Gerd lived with her family. Frey fell headlong in love with her and soon could not eat or sleep for thinking about her. This was a punishment from Odin for daring to sit on his throne, but when Njord learnt what had happened, he decided to help Frey.

It was too dangerous to send Frey himself to Jotunheim and so Njord sent his servant Skirnir to woo Gerd on Frey's behalf. Skirnir took with him Frey's magic sword, which could move through the air by itself, and his magic horse, which could see in the dark and gallop through the icy flames which surrounded Gerd's home. When he reached Gerd, Skirnir offered her wealth and the golden apples of eternal youth, as well as Frey's love. But her heart was made of ice and she rejected him. Exasperated by her reaction, Skirnir finally threatened to kill her father, Gymir. At that she promised to meet Frey in nine days' time.

Skirnir hurried back to tell him and, to Frey's delight, Gerd kept her promise. When they met, Frey's love melted the ice in Gerd's heart and she became warm and loving. Their marriage was thought to symbolize the sun melting the ice in springtime and allowing the earth to become warm and produce crops again.

ODIN STEALS THE MEAD OF POETRY

When the Aesir and Vanir gods made peace with each other after their quarrel, they sealed their agreement by all spitting into a huge jar. From this spittle a large man, called Kvasir, was formed. Although he was as big as a Giant, he was gentle. He was also very wise as he had inherited wisdom from each of the gods.

Unfortunately, two of the Dwarfs were jealous of his wisdom and wanted to steal it for themselves. They invited Kvasir to a feast and then murdered him. His blood filled three cauldrons and the Dwarfs mixed it with honey to make a special mead. Anyone who drank it would be inspired to write poetry, which was a gift that the Vikings valued very highly.

Knowing this mead was very precious, the Dwarfs guarded it carefully. One day, however, they made the mistake of murdering one of the relations of the Giant Suttungr. He went to the Dwarfs, intending to kill them in vengeance for the murder, but when they offered him the mead, he took that instead and spared their lives. Suttungr then hid the three cauldrons of mead deep inside a mountain and set his daughter, Gunnlod to guard them. But he could not resist boasting about what had happened and, when the gods heard about it, they decided they wanted the mead for themselves. Disguised as a handsome Giant by the name of Bolverk, Odin caused a quarrel between the nine men who worked for Suttungr's brother, Baugi. When the men had killed each other, Odin offered to take their place for the summer, asking only for a drink of mead as his wages. Baugi agreed, but at the end of the summer Suttungr refused to allow Odin his drink. Angry, Odin forced Baugi to tell him where the mead was hidden and, turning himself into a snake, sneaked inside the mountain through a tiny hole. Turning himself back into the handsome Bolverk, he started flattering Gunnlod. She soon fell in love with him and, after three nights, was persuaded to give him three sips of the mead. With each sip, Odin emptied a cauldron. He then turned himself into an eagle and flew back to Asgard, where the gods had three new cauldrons waiting for him. Odin spat one-third of the mead into each and later used it to give the gift of poetry to specially chosen humans.

THE TWILIGHT OF THE GODS

The Vikings believed that their gods would eventually be killed in a fierce battle against the Giants. Before this happened, however, there would be war among humans and Midgard itself would freeze over. The only people to escape death at this time would be a man and a woman, called Lif and Lifthrasir, who managed to shelter in the branches of Yggdrasil.

The sun and the moon would then be swallowed by the huge wolves, Skoll and Hati, who had been chasing them across the skies since the creation of the world. The stars would go out and Midgard would plunge into darkness.

The wicked Loki would escape from the cave where he had been imprisoned after Aegir's feast and join forces with the wolf, Fenrir. They would then join up with the Giants and the fiery beings from Muspell to attack Asgard. The rainbow bridge, Bifrost, would be destroyed and all the monsters would escape, but Heimdall, the guardian of Bifrost, would survive to warn the Nine Realms of the forthcoming battle, known as Ragnarok.

This battle world take place on a great plain, known as Vigard, and here the gods and their enemies would fight to the death. Odin would be accompanied by his sons and all the dead Vikings from Valhalla. In spite of this great army of experienced warriors, however, he would be killed and eaten by Fenrir. Odin's son, Vidar, would then kill Fenrir while Loki and Heimdall killed each other. Jormungand, the giant sea serpent, would come out of the sea and attack Thor who would kill him, but die of his poison.

After the battle, Surt, the guardian of Muspell, would destroy Asgard and Midgard by fire and the Nine Realms would sink into the sea. At first it would seem that only Yggdrasil had survived, but slowly land would rise from the sea, and the sun's daughter would come to warm the new earth. Plants and animals would reappear and Lif and Lifthrasir would come down from the branches of Yggdrasil to start the human race again.

Native Americans

Introduction

Native Americans believed that supernatural power was all around them – not just in living things like animals and birds, but also in trees, mountains, and rivers, in the sun, moon, and stars, in thunder, wind, and rain. Myths helped to explain much of what people found puzzling or frightening. In an environment which was often harsh and unpredictable they helped people to understand the forces which affected their lives, and why good or bad events happened. They described how the world began, why things came to be as they are and how the balance of nature should be maintained.

THE CREATION OF THE WORLD

In the beginning, people lived in the sky. The world below was covered by a vast expanse of water and only fish and birds lived there.

One day one of the Sky People, a young woman, became ill. Her brothers, hearing that a powerful medicine was buried under an ancient apple tree, carried her there. They laid Sky Woman down beside the tree and began to dig.

For hours they worked, until there was a deep crater around the tree, but still no medicine was found. All at once, with a noise like thunder, the edges of the crater gave way. The brothers scrambled to safety; but to their horror both the tree and Sky Woman fell into the crater and vanished from sight.

Two swans gliding on the ocean below heard the distant rumble and looked up to see the tree and the woman tumbling from the sky. Hastily spreading their wings they caught Sky Woman on their backs. A moment later, the apple tree crashed into the water beside them and sank into the depths. The swans turned their long necks and gazed at Sky Woman in astonishment.

"Who is it?" they whispered to one another. "Where has she come from? What shall we do with her?"

They sought the advice of the Big Turtle, oldest and wisest of all the creatures. Big Turtle stretched his neck from his shell and peered at Sky Woman, while the other animals and birds waited expectantly.

After much thought Big Turtle spoke, slowly and gravely: "The swans cannot carry their burden for ever," he said. "We must make an island where she can live. We can build it from the earth clinging to the roots of the apple tree and I will support it on my back. Who will go and find some earth for me?"

Otter, Muskrat and Beaver volunteered and, one by one, they dived down to look for the sunken tree. They were gone for a long time, but when they reappeared, tired and gasping, none of them had found a trace of it. It seemed as if Big Turtle's idea was doomed to failure.

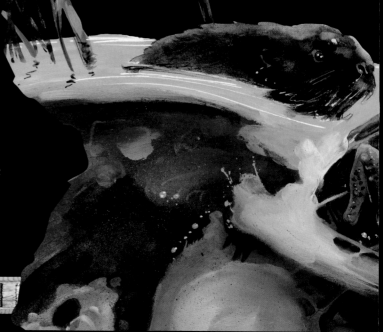

Suddenly, another voice piped up. "Let me go! I'll find some earth for you!"

It was Toad and, before anyone could stop her, she had disappeared. The other creatures shook their heads in disbelief at her foolishness. How could small, insignificant Toad hope to succeed where the best swimmers had failed?

Toad was gone for a very long time and the waiting animals feared the worst. But, at long last, her head broke the surface and she spat a mouthful of earth onto Big Turtle's shell before sinking back exhausted.

All the creatures set to work spreading the earth over Big Turtle's shell and, as they worked, the island grew until it was

big enough for Sky Woman to step ashore. The island continued to grow until it became the world where we live today, which, some people say, is still carried on Big Turtle's back.

RAVEN AND THE FIRST HUMAN BEINGS

The world was newly made. Raven flew over land and sea and admired what he had helped to create. He soared above forests and mountains where deer grazed among the trees and goats scrambled over the rocks. Gliding over streams and rivers, he saw beavers at work on their dams and glimpsed the silver flash of a leaping salmon. He swooped low over the ocean and saw that it teemed with fish and shellfish of every kind. Raven flew down and landed on a narrow strip of beach. He folded his wings and looked about him with satisfaction. The sun shone and the sea sparkled. Seals and sea lions basked on nearby rocks. Sea birds wheeled high overhead and in the distance, far out to sea, a whale spouted.

Suddenly, Raven's sharp eyes caught a slight movement by his feet. Bending down, he saw a stream of small bubbles escaping from something half-buried in the wet sand. It was a large clamshell and, as Raven watched, it began very slowly to open. From inside there came a faint sighing and murmuring, like a breeze ruffling the surface of the sea. To his amazement, Raven saw a little face craning forward, peering cautiously around. Then it caught sight of Raven

and, with a startled gasp, shot back inside the shell, which snapped shut once more. Raven hopped around the clamshell and examined it from all sides. He prodded it with his beak. The shell remained tightly closed. Raven tapped it impatiently. "Come out!" he whispered, "Come out!" Very gradually, the shell opened a fraction and the little face peeped out again. This time it was followed by another little face, then another and another, until there were a whole row of faces, gazing at Raven half in fear and half in wonder. As the shell opened a little more, Raven saw that it was full of little people – the very first human beings!

With Raven nodding encouragement, they slowly uncurled themselves from the depths of the clamshell and stepped out onto the sand. They stretched their arms and legs in the warm sunshine and whispered excitedly to one another as they looked around at the strange new world in which they found themselves. Raven was elated by his discovery. He told the human beings that, because they had been born on the shore, they belonged to both the sea and the land. Before he flew away, he taught them how to fish and how to work wood so that they could make their livelihood

from the riches around them. The human beings increased in number and spread all along the Northwest coast, making their homes along the shore between the sea and the forest-clad mountains. Thanks to Raven's teaching, they became successful fishermen and skilful woodcarvers and grew wealthy and powerful as a result.

COYOTE AND WOLF

When the world first began, the only inhabitants were animals. These animals were not the ones familiar to us today. They were bigger, stronger, and cleverer, and some of them looked different too. Bear, for example, had a long tail until Coyote tricked him into dipping it in an icy stream and it was frozen off. Coyote himself once had beautiful blue fur, but his pride caused him to fall in the dust, and so coyotes have been dust-colored ever since.

Many of these animals behaved just as human beings do now. They wore clothes and lived in houses, they went hunting and fishing and they fought with one another. They even looked like human beings sometimes, for they could change into any shape they had a mind to. When the real human beings came along later, animals changed into the ones we know now.

The two most important animals were Wolf and his younger brother, Coyote. Between them they helped to shape the world as it is today. Wolf did this because he wanted to make the world happy and pleasant, but Coyote, who was foolish and deceitful, usually did it by mistake or as a practical joke.

Unfortunately, Coyote's tricks often backfired, leaving him a sadder, though not always wiser, animal.

In the beginning, for example, Wolf had wanted death to be only temporary, so that when people died they could be brought back to life again. Coyote, just to be difficult, argued against this and so it was agreed that death should be final. When Coyote's own son died, he begged Wolf to change this rule, but Wolf refused, pointing out that it was Coyote who had insisted on it in the first place.

Sometimes Coyote's trickery brought good results. Crane had stolen all the fire in the world for himself, so that the other animals had no means of cooking or keeping warm. Coyote disguised himself with a wig made from reeds and stole into Crane's camp at night while there was a dance going on. Joining in unnoticed, Coyote danced nearer and nearer the fire and, at the right moment, dipped his wig into the flames. The dry reeds caught alight instantly and Coyote dashed off into the night, carrying aloft his wig, now blazing like a torch. The other animals helped him to carry the fire all over the country so that now everyone can benefit from it.

THE ACORN HATS

According to some Californian tribes, the first people to inhabit the world were the Ikxareyavs. They prepared the way for human beings and became the animals, birds, and plants which exist today.

For several days, wisps of smoke had been seen on the distant mountains. The Ikxareyavs knew that this heralded the appearance of human beings. Everyone rushed to prepare for the new arrivals.

The Acorn Girls were hard at work weaving new caps for the occasion. The two elder sisters, Maul Oak Girl and Black Oak Girl, were both skilful weavers. They deftly twisted and knotted hazel shoots, pine roots, grass, and fern stems into intricate patterns of gold and brown and black. Tan Oak Girl, the youngest sister, was not such a good weaver. She was slow and clumsy and try as she might, the twigs and shoots would not bend as pliantly or lie as smoothly as her awkward fingers wished. She was aware of her sisters' scorn and her cheeks reddened as she overheard their mocking whispers and laughter.

Almost together, with whoops of triumph, Maul Oak Girl and Black Oak Girl bounded to their feet, their finished caps on their heads. The caps were very beautiful, well-shaped, and finely woven, and the two girls turned this way and that, admiring each other.

"Now we are ready to go!" declared Maul Oak Girl. "We must hurry if we are to get to the woods in time."

"Please don't go without me!" cried Tan Oak Girl. "Please wait! Look – I've almost finished!" And she turned her cap inside out to trim off the loose ends.

"We can't wait," the others called. "If you aren't ready, we must leave you behind."

Tan Oak Girl hastily crammed on her cap, still inside out, and ran after them. When her sisters saw her cap, with untrimmed spikes of grass and twigs sticking out all over it, they burst out laughing. "What a sight you are!" they cried. "The human beings won't want anything to do with you!" Suddenly they stopped, for the

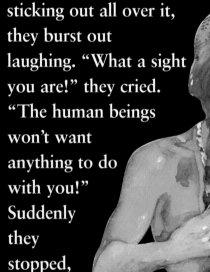

human beings had just arrived and had heard their cruel words.

The human beings spoke kindly to Tan Oak Girl. "Although your cap is not as pretty as the others," they said, "you will provide the best food and because of you, people will never go hungry."

Shy and embarrassed, Tan Oak Girl hid her face inside her cap. Her sisters, overcome with shame, did the same. They grew smaller and smaller until they turned into the acorns we know today. Tan Oak acorns still have rough and prickly caps, but they taste the best and people prefer them to acorns like those of Maul Oak and Black Oak which are harder to pound into flour and not as good to eat.

135

THE BOY WHO WAS KEPT BY A BEAR

A boy, lost in the forest, was found by a bear, who took pity on him and adopted him as his own son. He cared for the boy throughout the summer, teaching him to hunt and fish and showing him where

the bees kept their honey and where the best berries grew. When autumn came, he took the boy up into the mountains to his winter den. It was warm and dry and the bear kept it well stocked with food.

The boy's father had never lost hope of finding his son. He looked for him each time he went hunting and it so happened that, as the first snows of winter began to fall, his footsteps took him toward the bear's den. Although he was still far distant, the bear sensed his approach and resolved to use all his powers to distract him from his quest.

Taking a porcupine carcass from his larder, he threw it out of the den. At that very moment, many miles away, the hunter noticed where a porcupine had gnawed a tree by the forest track. He thought of pursuing the animal, but decided instead to leave it for the time being and continued on his way.

The bear next threw out a beaver carcass, just as the distant hunter was passing a lake. The man noticed that some beavers had built a lodge there and made a note to set a trap on his way back.

Finally the bear threw out a partridge and at that very instant a partridge whirred across the hunter's path. Again he

was tempted to follow the bird, but again he decided to return for it later.

As a last resort the bear conjured up a fierce storm of howling wind and whirling snow, but still the boy's father struggled on, every step bringing him closer and closer to the bear's den.

The bear groaned in despair, "I cannot defeat him! He is walking straight to me!" The boy tried to comfort him, but the bear said, "Do not be sad. I know that I am soon to die, but I can still help you to become a mighty hunter. When I am dead, cut off one of my forelegs and wrap it up in soft buckskin. Keep this bundle hanging up in your tent above the place where you always sit. When you want to hunt bear, find a spot from where you can survey the whole countryside and look for a place where smoke is rising. Only you will be able see this and there you will always find a bear."

At that moment the boy's father broke through the snow covering the entrance to the bear's den. The bear went to meet him and was killed. The boy returned home with his father, but he never forgot the bear. He kept his friend's foreleg just as he had been told and grew up to be a very successful hunter.

THE BUFFALO DANCE

For many weeks no buffalo had been sighted on the Plains and people were starving. Early one morning, a girl went to fetch water from the river. To her surprise, she saw a herd of buffalo grazing peacefully on a nearby bluff, almost directly above a corral.

"Oh, buffalo!" she cried joyfully. "If you will only jump into the corral, I will marry one of you!"

She turned to alert the camp's hunters, but before she could move she heard the thundering of hoofs and saw the whole herd plunge over the edge of the bluff into the corral below. One great bull escaped and bounded toward her. She tried to escape, but the buffalo seized her and tossed her on his back.

"You promised to marry one of us if we jumped," he reminded her. "Now you will be my wife."

In vain the girl protested that she had only been joking. Unheeding, the buffalo carried her away over the prairie.

Her father set out to look for her and, after many miles came to a muddy waterhole. A herd of buffalo was grazing a little way off. To his delight, he saw his daughter coming toward him.

"I cannot return home with you," said the girl. "I have been sent for water and if I run away, the buffalo will follow and kill us both."

No sooner had she spoken than the buffalo herd was upon them. Snorting in fury, they trampled the man into the mud with their cruel hoofs so that not a trace of him remained.

"You see now how it is for us," said the buffalo. "So many of us have been killed by your people for food. But we will give you a chance. If you can restore your father to life, you may both return home."

As the girl sat weeping by the water hole, a magpie flew down beside her.

"Oh, please help me!" begged the girl. "Help me find my father's body."

The magpie jabbed the mud around the waterhole with his beak, and at last he pulled out a tiny piece of bone. The girl laid the bone on the ground and covered it with her buffalo robe. She began to sing and pray and such was the power of her songs and prayers that her father returned to life. When she lifted the robe, he stood up unharmed.

The buffalo were amazed. "You have strong powers," they said. "Now we will teach you our dance and song. You must never forget them."

When the girl and her

father returned home, they taught their people the buffalos' song and their slow, stately dance. This was how the warrior society called the Buffalo Bulls came into being and why they dance wearing the skins and heads of the buffalo.

THE SEARCH FOR THE CORN SISTERS

In the beginning the first people had only grass seeds to eat and, because they were always hungry, they begged the Seed People to send them something more. The Seed People took pity on them and sent them the six beautiful Corn Sisters.

In their blankets of purest white, edged with all the colors of the rainbow, the Corn Sisters moved gracefully through the grass and, as they moved, the plants grew tall and strong, bearing long leaves and silken tassels. The Corn Sisters gently peeled back the leaves and the people saw for the first time the six colors of corn – yellow, blue, red, white, speckled, and black.

For many years the Corn Sisters lived among the first people and were loved and honored by them for their goodness and kindness. In time, however, because the corn was so plentiful, the people became wasteful. They allowed weeds to choke their fields. They tore the ripe cobs roughly from the plants and shelled the corn carelessly so that much of it was trampled underfoot. They ground more corn meal than they needed and threw away what they did not use. They no longer showed the Corn Sisters respect.

At last the Corn Sisters could endure no more. Drawing their blankets over their heads, they left the village and fled to the home of the Kachinas high in the mountains. The Kachinas, angered by their story, hid them at the bottom of a lake where the people would not be able to find them.

At first, the people paid little heed. They continued to squander their corn so that when planting time came, very little seed corn remained. They sowed what they had, but the plants were sickly and the few ears harvested were pale and shrivelled. The following harvest was worse and the next failed entirely.

Now the people were starving. They wanted to ask the Corn Sisters to forgive them and return, but they did not know where they had gone. They sent out messengers, but no one could find them. At last they begged the help of Paiyatuma, the flute-player, who, since the world began, had brought the dew and mists of dawn to freshen the earth and the growing plants.

Realizing that the people had learnt a bitter lesson, Paiyatuma agreed to their desperate pleas. He began to play and, as his music soared, it drew the Corn Sisters from the lake. The people welcomed them back joyfully, and all that day, as Paiyatuma played his flute, the Corn Sisters

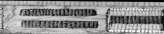

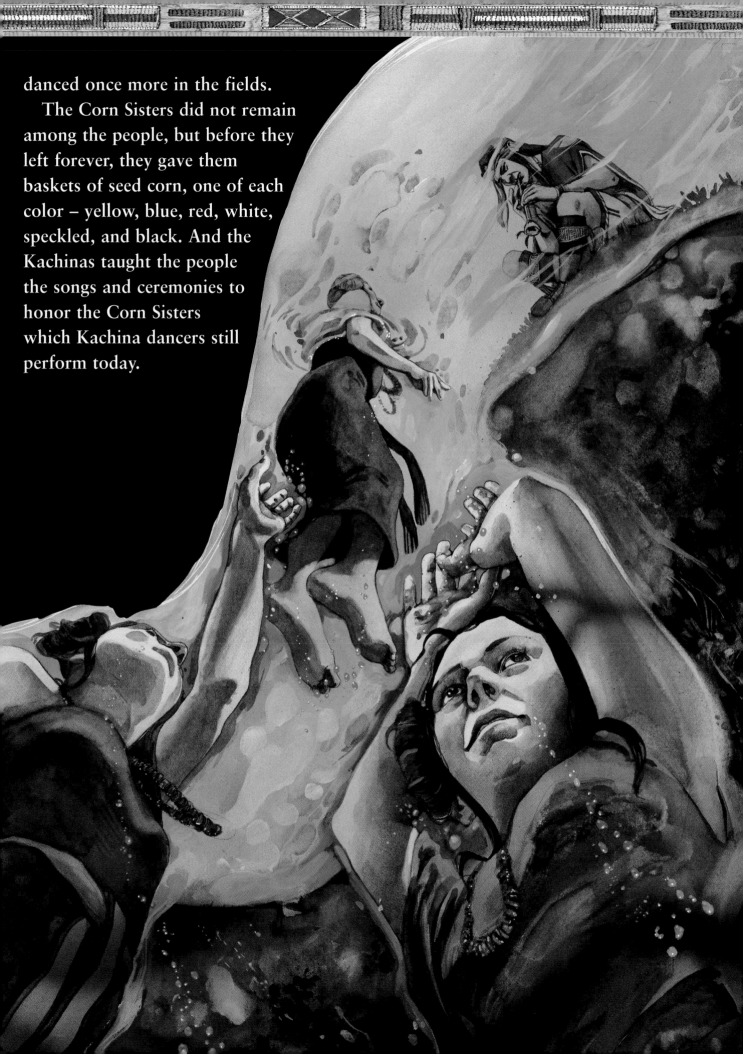

danced once more in the fields.

The Corn Sisters did not remain among the people, but before they left forever, they gave them baskets of seed corn, one of each color – yellow, blue, red, white, speckled, and black. And the Kachinas taught the people the songs and ceremonies to honor the Corn Sisters which Kachina dancers still perform today.

THE RAIN CHANT

A hunter, who had stopped by a river to rest from the midday sun, was surprised to see a baby girl swimming in the water. He returned at the same time for several days and again found the baby swimming there. One day, going earlier than usual, he hid in the reeds by the water's edge. As he watched, the baby rose to the surface and floated toward the bank. The hunter snatched her up and ran away as fast as he could. He stopped for a moment to look back and saw the river raging like a whirlpool. He ran on, not stopping until he got home.

The hunter and his wife adopted the child as their own daughter. When she was older, they told her how she had been found and the girl decided to visit the place. As she approached the river, she heard someone chopping wood. When she reached the bank, however, the sound stopped and there was no one there. She returned to the river next day, and again the following day, and each time the same thing happened.

On the fourth day, her foster-father said to her sadly, "I realize now that I stole you from the Holy People who live in the river. These offerings will ease your journey back to your old home."

He gave her a basket filled with precious stones and shells, sprinkled with pollen and river crystals and once more the girl returned to the river. This time, a young man was standing on the bank. He frowned when he saw the girl.

"Why are you here?" he demanded. "This is the home of the Water Buffalo and no place for Earth Surface People."

The girl told her story and the young man nodded. "You must be the Water Buffalo baby who disappeared long ago," he said. "Follow me." And, rolling back the river like a blanket, he led her to the home of the Water Buffalo.

The Water Buffalo was large and imposing, with the horns and hoofs of a buffalo and the mane and tail of a horse. He welcomed the girl and accepted her basket of offerings graciously.

"I am glad that you have come," said the Water Buffalo. "I have something to give you before you return to the Earth Surface forever." And he gave her a little buckskin bag tied with a thong. "Your people must use this when they want rain. It contains the four winds and four mists, together with hair cut from my mane and mud from the river."

Then the Water Buffalo taught the girl the songs and prayers needed to bring rain, and showed her how to build the special hogan for the rain ceremony and how to decorate it with plants and flowers.

When the girl returned home, she remembered everything the Water Buffalo had told her. She and her descendants became known as the Meeting of the Rivers People, who knew how to bring rain.

THE PLEIADES

There were once seven boys who spent all their time playing chunkey and gambling. Every morning they gathered at the chunk yard, an area of level sand near the townhouse.

As soon as the chunkey stone was rolled along the ground, two of the boys hurled their poles after it, each attempting to hit it or prevent the other from doing so. Their friends cheered from the sidelines, counting up the scores and making bets on the outcome of the match. All day long the boys played this game, stopping only when darkness fell.

In vain their mothers reminded them of the work to be done in the fields – the planting, hoeing, and weeding, and all the labor of harvest. They pleaded, shouted, and scolded, but to no avail. There was nothing that could drag those boys away from the chunkey game. Finally, their mothers lost patience with them and decided to teach them a lesson.

That evening the boys returned home as usual for supper. Mouth-watering aromas filled the air and they took their places eagerly, expecting to find their bowls filled with delicious corn stew. Instead, the bowls contained nothing but chunkey stones. Mystified, they looked round. Everyone was laughing at them.

"What do you expect?" asked their mothers, smiling grimly. "Since you would rather play at chunkey than help us, you can feast on chunkey stones!"

Angry and resentful at the trick played on them, the boys rushed back to the chunk yard. They decided that they would leave home. They danced around the townhouse, slowly at first, then with gathering speed. Round and round they whirled, faster and faster, until their feet left the ground. As they rose into the air, their mothers tried to catch them, but the boys were beyond their reach. One of the mothers managed to pull her son down by hooking a chunkey pole into his belt, but he landed with such force that he sank into the ground and the earth closed over him.

The other boys soared higher until they were no more than pinpoints of light in the night sky. They became the cluster of stars known as the Pleiades and they are there in the heavens still.

The mother of the boy who sank into the earth visited the spot each day, watering it with her tears. A little green shoot appeared and grew into a tall pine tree. People said that it was the seventh boy, trying to rejoin his lost companions. The pine tree has never been able to reach the Pleiades, but its wood burns brightly and gives off sparks like shooting stars.

THE FLOATING ISLAND

When the Algonkian hero Glooskap first arrived, the world was not as it is today. Animals were larger and stronger than they are now. The moose, tall as a mountain, trampled everything in its path. The squirrel tore down trees with its teeth, destroying whole forests in a single day. Knowing that the world could not survive if this persisted, Glooskap shrank the animals to their present sizes.

For a time all went well until one day the river, which served the whole country with pure clear water, ran dry. A greedy water monster had swallowed it all up. The monster was so huge that its body filled the whole river valley. Its mouth was a mile wide, its eyes stuck out like pine knots and its bloated body was covered with huge warts. When Glooskap went to demand the water back, the monster opened its gaping mouth to swallow him up. But Glooskap made himself taller than the tallest pine tree and seized the monster in his huge hand. He squeezed until he had wrung every drop of water from it so that the river ran freely again. Glooskap stayed to help and protect the world for thousands of years and during that time only one person managed to

defeat him. While on a journey, Glooskap stopped to rest at a tipi. On the floor of the tipi sat a baby, smiling and crowing. Glooskap had never seen such a creature before and he ordered the baby to come to him. The baby laughed, but did not move. Glooskap frowned and then shouted at the baby, but it only began to howl loudly and Glooskap rushed from the tipi in despair. When babies today say "Goo-goo!", they are remembering how one of their number defeated the mighty Glooskap long, long ago.

One day, seabirds brought Glooskap news of a mysterious island drifting toward the shore. The excited birds told him that there were three tall trees on the island with strange creatures climbing among the branches. Glooskap shook his head sadly, for he had already learnt in a dream that this was no island, but a three-masted sailing ship manned by pale-skinned strangers. Their arrival would bring many changes and he decided to take his leave. He set out in his birchbark canoe, the desolate cries of the seabirds mourning his departure. It is said that he lives on still, somewhere at the edge of the world, and will come again, when the time is right, to help and protect the world.

ANCIENT
CHINESE

INTRODUCTION

The beginnings of Chinese civilization have been traced back to the Yellow River region. As the population of China grew, many small farming settlements joined together. Gradually, these villages developed into towns and cities, where power was held by ruling families. These families became known as dynasties, and some believe that the first dynasties were founded as early as 2200 BC. Under the influence of different dynasties and religions, Chinese mythology and civilization developed into a rich mixture of ancient beliefs, new discoveries, and traditional learning. Many important inventions that are widely used today were first developed in ancient China, including the compass, the seismograph, and clockwork.

PAN GU CREATES THE WORLD

At the very beginning, the universe was dark chaos in the shape of a round egg. It was not separated into heaven and earth, or day and night. The great giant, Pan Gu, slept curled up in the chaos. He lay there fast asleep for 18,000 years, all the time growing larger and larger. Then Pan Gu woke up. Because he was not satisfied with the chaos surrounding him, Pan Gu broke the eggshell open with an axe and a chisel.

As a result, the universe changed greatly. The light, clear matter rose and became heaven, and the thick, heavy matter sank and formed the earth. Pan Gu was worried that heaven and earth might join together, so he stood in the middle, holding up heaven with his head to keep it separate from the earth.

Every day during this period, heaven rose one zhang (equal to 11 feet 9 inches), earth grew one zhang, and Pan Gu also grew one zhang. This growth ceased after another 18,000 years. By this time Pan Gu was extremely tall, and the distance between heaven and earth was 90,000 li (equal to about 30,000 miles.) Pan Gu stood there alone, stopping heaven and earth from joining and collapsing back into chaos.

Many years passed. Pan Gu, who had been holding heaven up for a long time, felt very tired. Eventually, he lay down on the earth and died. His breath turned into winds and clouds; his voice became thunder; his left eye changed into the sun, and his right eye became the moon; his hair and beard transformed into stars; his arms and legs formed the four corners of the earth; and his body became the Five Sacred Mountains (the five most famous mountains in China).

Pan Gu's blood became flowing rivers; his veins turned into roads and paths; his muscles became fertile lands; his skin and fine hair changed into flourishing woods, grass, and beautiful flowers; his teeth and bones became metals and stones; his bone marrow became pearls and jades; and his sweat became rain and dew moistening the earth. And this is how a world that was suitable for human beings to live in was created.

Nü Wa Creates the Human Race

After the creation of heaven and earth, there were mountains and rivers, plains and trees, birds and animals, insects and fish – but there were no people. There was only the beautiful goddess Nü Wa.

Nü Wa felt very lonely, and one day while she was walking around on the earth, she wondered what she could add to the world to make it more lively. When she grew tired, she rested by the edge of a pond. She glanced into the water and saw her own reflection – then it struck her. She would make some living creatures that looked like her.

Nü Wa dug up some yellow earth next to the pond, and blended it with a little water. Using this mixture, she made a small creature that looked like her own image in the water. She put the little clay figure on the earth, and as it touched the soil, it came to life. Nü Wa named it Ren, meaning "human being".

Nü Wa was very satisfied with her work. She made one person after another. With all these little human beings around her, she no longer felt so lonely. Nü Wa hoped to make so many of them that they could spread all over the vast land. She worked until sunset and then started work again at dawn the following day. But Nü Wa grew very tired. Then she thought of a quicker way to work. She dipped a cane stem into the muddy water, and flicked it over the land. The little clay drops also became human beings.

Using this simple method, Nü Wa completed her task quickly. The humans she had shaped herself became the rich people, while those made from mud splashes became the poor. In order to continue the life of the human race, Nü Wa divided the people into men and women so they could produce their own children. In this way, the human race soon spread all over the world.

THE EIGHT IMMORTALS

155

The Eight Immortals were close friends and always spent a lot of time traveling, playing, and enjoying adventures together. The Heavenly Empress, Hsi Wang–mu, threw a party once every 3,000 years, following the harvest of the peaches of immortality. After one of these very special parties, the Eight Immortals were too tired to ride home on the clouds, as they usually did, in case they fell off. So they decided to cross the seas instead.

They all floated safely on the waters, using magic objects as rafts; Chung–li rode on his feather fan, and Ti Guai Li rode on his iron cane. But the son of the Dragon King, who lived under the sea, became fascinated with the magic flute that Lan Ts'ai–ho was playing as she floated on her jade board. He sucked her down into the depths of the waters and stole her flute.

When the other seven Immortals realized that Lan was being held prisoner under the waves, they threatened to destroy the palace of the Dragon King unless she was freed immediately. But the Dragon King's son refused, and so a great battle began. In their anger, the Immortals lit huge fires, and the heat and flames burned the seas dry.

The friends found Lan and rescued her, but although they searched everywhere, they could not find her flute. Lan was filled with grief at losing her precious instrument, but the Immortals were running out of time as the Dragon King's warriors quickly poured water back into the sea basin in an effort to drown their attackers.

Just in time, the Immortals escaped to dry land. They were even more furious now, and used all their strength to topple an enormous mountain into the sea so that it wouldn't hold any more water. The battle raged on, until eventually the Dragon King's son was killed and the Immortals managed to recover Lan's flute, which he had been hiding. Then the Jade Emperor sent his Heavenly Guards down to make peace between the Dragon King and the Eight Immortals, and finally the fighting ceased.

YAN DI, GOD OF AGRICULTURE AND MEDICINE

Yan Di (Lord Radiant) was a kind god. His head was like that of an ox, and he had a human body. As the number of people on the earth grew, there were no longer enough wild plants growing naturally to feed everybody. The people risked going hungry. When Yan Di saw this, he taught them how to cultivate the land and grow their own crops, to help them provide food for themselves.

As Yan Di was teaching the people, many grain seeds fell from the sky. Yan Di taught people how to sow these seeds in plowed fields. He made the sun to give enough light and heat for the crops to grow. The people finally had enough food to eat, and even some left over to store. They called Yan Di the Holy Farmer, or the God of Agriculture, to show their gratitude for his help.

Yan Di was also the God of Medicine. He had a magic red whip, and by using it to strike an herb plant, Yan Di could tell whether the plant was poisonous or not, and whether the plant's nature was basically hot or cold. In this way, he could find the right herbs to cure people's illnesses. But to find out exactly what effect certain herbs had, Yan Di tasted them himself. It was said that he was transparent, so if he tasted a poisonous herb, he could tell which part of his body was affected and use another herb to cure himself. Once, Yan Di was poisoned seventy times in just one day.

Eventually he died from eating a poisonous herb – some say it was called "Bowel-Breaking Weed," while others say it was the "Hundred–Legged Vermin" plant that killed him. But whichever plant it was, he sacrificed himself for the good of human beings – so they would know which plants were medicinal and which were poisonous.

In addition to teaching people how to farm and how to treat their illnesses, Yan Di also taught them how to make farming tools and pottery, and helped them create the calendar.

WEAVING MAID AND COWHERD

Weaving Maid was a grandchild of the Emperor of Heaven. In heaven, she and her sisters wove beautiful colored clouds for the sky called "celestial garments." They changed color depending on what time of day and season it was.

At that time the Milky Way was the Silver River, and it lay in between heaven and earth. Cowherd and his old cow lived a lonely life on earth, on the other side of the Silver River. One day, the cow suddenly started to speak. She told Cowherd that the beautiful Weaving Maid was coming with other fairies to swim in the river. If Cowherd stole Weaving Maid's clothes while she was swimming, he could then marry her.

Cowherd went to the Silver River. Just as the cow said, Weaving Maid and her sisters came to the Milky Way, took off their silk gowns, and dived into the river. Cowherd grabbed Weaving Maid's clothes and refused to return them unless she agreed to marry him. Weaving Maid agreed.

The two were married secretly and lived a very happy life together.

Weaving Maid wove cloth and Cowherd farmed the land. They loved each other very much and had two children: one boy and one girl.

But one day the Emperor and Empress of Heaven found out that their granddaughter had married a mere mortal. They were so enraged that they snatched back Weaving Maid and locked her up. The Queen of Heaven shifted the Silver River up to heaven (where it was called the Milky Way) so that Cowherd could not cross over from earth.

The old cow told Cowherd that when she died he should wrap himself in her skin and fly to heaven. This he did, carrying the children. When they were almost there, the Queen of Heaven changed the Milky Way into a raging river. Cowherd could not cross it. He and his children used spoons to try and ladle out the water from the Milky Way, hoping to empty it so they could cross.

The Emperor of Heaven was so moved by their love for his granddaughter that he ordered magpies to form a bridge across the Milky Way – they still do this on every July 4 of the lunar calendar so that Weaving Maid and Cowherd can meet on the bridge once a year.

KING YAO

Yao was a very kind and wise king. He lived a plain and simple life, and his home was a thatched shack. Yao always tried to help his subjects, and they loved him with all their hearts.

One day, many favorable omens appeared around Yao's home. A phoenix, a holy bird, flew into his courtyard; all the horse-feed turned into rice; and lucky grasses started to grow in the backyard. It was believed that all these good things showed that the gods in heaven were pleased by Yao's kindness and wisdom.

Besides being an excellent king, Yao had also chosen very competent ministers to help him rule and make decisions. His judge, Gao Tao, had a magic, one-horned goat that could tell the guilty from the innocent. During courtroom trials, Gao Tao would ask this special goat to butt one of the suspects with his horn. The goat always butted the person who had done wrong. But if the person was innocent, the goat would refuse. Gao Tao therefore never made any mistakes in his trials. The goat was extremely useful and honest, so Gao Tao cared for it very well.

Yao had other ministers with unusual powers. The Minister of Music, Kui, had only one leg. He made music by imitating the sounds of nature, which calmed and soothed everybody who heard it. He beat stones together to create rhythm. His music was so beautiful and entrancing that all the birds and animals loved to dance to it.

Once, a strong old man who lived on pine seeds came to Yao. He brought Yao some of the seeds, but Yao was too busy to eat them. It was said that those who ate the pine seeds lived to be 200 or 300 years old.

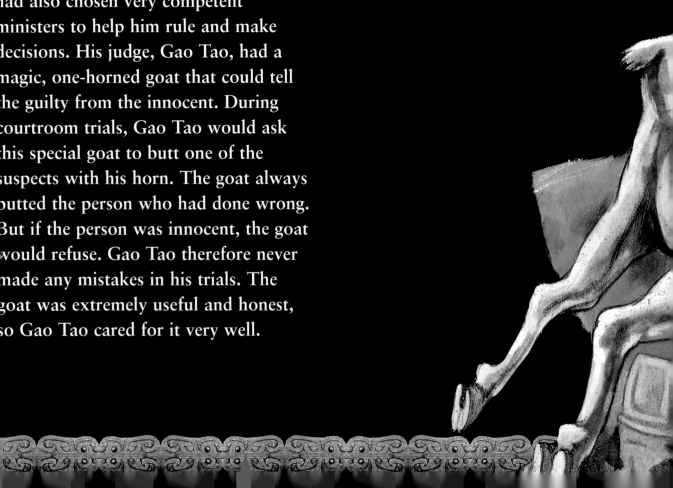

THE BATTLE BETWEEN HUANG DI AND CHI YOU

Huang Di was the supreme god of the universe and the God of the Center. He had four faces that pointed toward north, south, east, and west, so he could see what was happening in all directions, and no one could trick him or act behind his back. Huang Di was also the ruler of the ghost world.

In order to strengthen his ruling position, Huang Di fought a war with the god of the south, Yan Di, and defeated him. Later, Chi You, a descendant of Yan Di, led a rebellion of the Miao people in the south, assisted by the ghosts of the mountains and forests.

They fought a fierce battle with Huang Di's army in Zhuolu. Chi You had about 80 brothers. Every one of them had an iron–hard head, four eyes, and six hands, and was extraordinarily ferocious and strong. They also possessed various magical powers. At first, fighting against such superhuman warriors, Huang Di and the gods and beasts suffered several defeats.

At one point, in the middle of a battle, Chi You blew a thick fog from his nostrils. Huang Di and his troops became trapped in the heavy clouds and could not escape. They became confused, not knowing which way to flee, and many of them were killed. The Queen of Winds took pity on them and invented the "compass cart," a vehicle decorated with an iron figure that always pointed south, so that Huang Di's troops could finally find their way out of the blinding fog.

Huang Di had a dragon named Dragon Ying, which could spread rainstorms. Huang Di asked Dragon Ying to attack Chi You, but before he could do this, Chi You ordered the Duke of Winds and the Master of Rains to create gales and storms to scatter Huang Di's troops.

Now Huang Di sought help from the Celestial Lady Ba, and she sent out fierce heat to dry up the storms. After many intense wars, Huang Di killed all of Chi You's brothers. Chi You himself was captured alive, imprisoned in chains, and then executed. His blood-stained shackles later became a maple forest, and his blood dyed the trees a flaming red color.

THE TEN SUNS

A long time ago, there were ten suns. They were the sons of the Emperor of Heaven, and it was their duty to shine over the earth one at a time in an orderly fashion. But one day, during the period of King Yao's reign, these naughty children all appeared in the sky at the same time and danced around wildly.

The suns dried up all the crops in the soil, and people could hardly breathe in the heat. Even the witch who produced the rain died from too much sun. As well as creating serious drought, the severe heat also brought monsters out of the forests and swamps, and they attacked the people.

Yao, who loved his subjects as he loved his own sons, prayed to the Emperor of Heaven. The Emperor of Heaven sent one of his gods named Yi to help people on earth. He gave Yi a red bow and a bag of white arrows. Yi was a superb archer.

If he aimed at a target 100 times, he would hit it 100 times. He came to earth and shot dead all the fearsome monsters. Then Yi decided to get rid of those hateful suns and prepared ten arrows. At first he pretended to shoot at the suns, hoping that this might frighten them away. Yet they were not afraid. So Yi shot an arrow into the sky, and one sun exploded in a ball of fire. When it reached the earth, Yi saw that the sun had become a huge raven with three legs. After that, he shot down another eight suns.

Yao, who was watching beside Yi, thought that one sun would be useful to human beings. He asked his people to take away Yi's last arrow so that one sun was left in the sky. After that day, the remaining sun dared not misbehave. Every day it carries out its duty of providing light and heat for the world and disappears at night, allowing people to live, work, and sleep as normal.

It is said that the nine ravens fell into the ocean and formed a giant, scorching rock. Sea waters that crashed onto this rock evaporated. So even though water from all the rivers and streams flows into the sea, it never overflows.

THE FIRST SILKWORM

Once upon a time, there was a man who left his home to travel to a faraway place, leaving behind his little daughter and his horse.

The girl took good care of the horse, but she felt very lonely because her father had been away for a long time.

One day, the girl spoke jokingly to the horse: "If you could bring my father home, I would marry you." When it heard her words, the horse wrenched itself free from its tether and ran off to find her father. After several days he found him and neighed sadly, looking in the direction of home.

The father immediately imagined that something terrible had happened to the girl. He quickly mounted the horse to return to his daughter, and they were joyfully reunited. Of course, he did not know why the horse had come for him. He simply thought that the animal was clever and loyal.

So the man offered his horse good feed and cared for him well. But the horse did not want to eat anything, and every time he saw the little girl, he jumped up and down and neighed. The father thought that this was rather strange. When he asked his daughter about the horse's behavior, she confessed the promise she had made to the horse.

The father was angry and said it was impossible that a human being should marry an animal. With his bow and arrow he shot the horse dead. He laid the skin on the ground outside in the sun to dry. One day, when the father was not at home, his daughter and her friends were playing together near the horsehide. Suddenly, the hide jumped up from the ground, wrapped itself tightly around the girl, and disappeared with her. A few days later, her father found her in a mulberry tree. The girl wrapped in the horsehide had become a silkworm, spinning silk in the tree. This is the origin of the silkworm.

Printed in China